what really counts

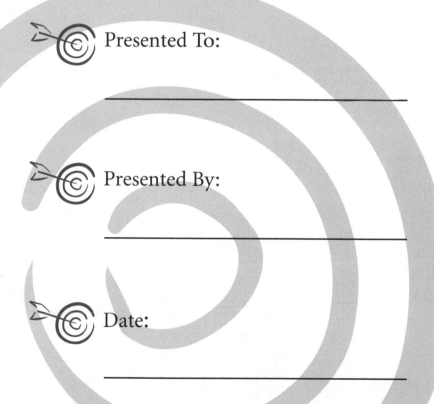

Presented To:

_____

Presented By:

_____

Date:

_____

what
really
counts

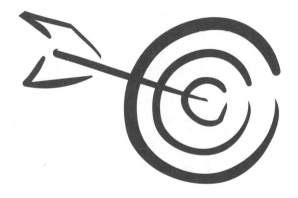

NELSON BOOKS
A Division of Thomas Nelson Publishers
Since 1798

www.thomasnelson.com

Published in Nashville, Tennessee, by Thomas Nelson, Inc.

Scripture quotations noted ESV are from The Holy Bible, English Standard Version, copyright © 2001 by Crossway Bibles, a division of Good News Publishers. Used by permission. All rights reserved. • Scripture quotations noted NKJV are from THE NEW KING JAMES VERSION. Copyright © 1979, 1980, 1982, Thomas Nelson, Inc., Publishers. • Scripture quotations noted KJV are from the KING JAMES VERSION. • Scripture quotations noted NASB are taken from the NEW AMERICAN STANDARD BIBLE®, © Copyright The Lockman Foundation 1960, 1962, 1963, 1968, 1971, 1972, 1973, 1975, 1977, 1995. Used by permission. • Scripture quotations noted NIV are from the HOLY BIBLE: NEW INTERNA-TIONAL VERSION®. Copyright © 1973, 1978, 1984 by International Bible Society. Used by permission of Zondervan Publishing House. All rights reserved. • Scripture quotations noted NLT are from the Holy Bible, New Living Translation, copyright © 1996. Used by permission of Tyndale House Publishers, Inc., Wheaton, Illinois 60189. All rights reserved. • Scripture quotations noted NCV are from the Holy Bible, New Century Version, copyright © 1987, 1988, 1991, by Word Publishing, a division of Thomas Nelson, Inc. All rights reserved. Used by permission.

Managing Editor: Lila Empson
Associate Editor: Kristen Lucas
Manuscript: Alton Gansky
Design: Thatcher Design, Nashville, TN

Library of Congress Cataloging-in-Publication Data

What really counts.
     p. cm.
  ISBN 0-7852-0926-3 (pbk.)
  1. Christian life. I. Thomas Nelson Publishers.
  BV4501.3.W44 2005
  248.4—dc22
                2005024935

It is not my ability, but my response to God's ability that counts.

CORRIE TEN BOOM

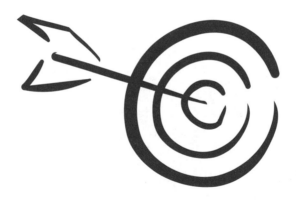

Contents

Introduction

> ### "I have a new philosophy.
> ### I'm only going to dread
> ### one day at a time."

Those insightful words came not from a philosopher but from cartoonist Charles M. Schulz. Interesting how something so profound can come from a made-up character like Charlie Brown. Many of us grew up with Charlie Brown and his pals from *Peanuts*. We have an affinity for the boy who always seemed just one step out of cadence with the march of humanity. Perhaps this is so because we often feel the same way.

In the real day-to-day struggle for meaning, success, and happiness, we find ourselves struggling to do it all, be it all, and take it all in. It's impossible. The things that demand our attention and time are annoyingly persistent. There is always another day of work, another soccer game to take the kids to, another business meeting to attend, a roof that needs to be fixed, a lawn that needs to be mowed, a car that needs to be washed, a tax form to be filled out, and a social engagement that requires our presence. At times we feel more like a Ping-Pong ball than a person, and we admire someone like Charlie Brown who has the discipline to dread only one day at a time.

What follows is an effort to help us understand what really counts in life. Some of the items will seem obvious, others may seem strange, but each is meant to help you get a handle on the important things. And if you do, you will be able to turn Charlie Brown's words around and say, "I have a new philosophy. I'm going to embrace every new day."

—Alton Gansky

LIFE

An Introduction

> We are confident, I say, and would prefer to be away from the body and at home with the Lord.
>
> 2 CORINTHIANS 5:8 NIV

A poet wrote some verses about life and death. Much of the poem is a series of questions:

what really counts

Not "How did he die?" But "How did he live?"

Not "What did he gain?" But "What did he give?"

For many, life is nothing more than the time we spend between birth and death. If we're lucky, we might have some happiness. Life is much more than that. Life begins at birth and, because of Jesus, can continue after death.

Most of us learn of death early in life. A grandparent dies, or a member of your neighbor's family. Death seems unnatural. It is. Nonetheless, it is real. Life takes meaning in death. What we do now lives long after us. We may accumulate wealth, but we forge memories.

Living is investing in others. It is the application of our skills or talents to whatever we find ourselves doing. Every morning we wake up—we all have that in common. What differs is what we do with each new morning, each new day. Knowing how to die without fear is a great achievement; knowing how to live without fear is an even greater work. Both are possible through Christ. It is our connection to God that makes death understandable. That's what the unknown poet meant when he ended his poem:

Not "What did the sketch in the newspaper say?"

But "How many were sorry when he passed away?"

Mark Twain quipped that we "should live our lives so that even the undertaker will be sorry when we die." There's good advice in that.

> Each small task of everyday life is part of the total harmony of the universe.
>
> SAINT THERESA OF LISIEUX

Life

Life After Life

To me, to live is Christ,
and to die is gain.
PHILIPPIANS 1:21 NKJV

what really counts

Statisticians love numbers. They count and use high-powered formulas to describe the world. They have learned something important: For every 100 people counted, 100 will someday die. The truth may seem obvious, but many people go to great lengths to avoid the subject.

Sarah Winchester built a remarkable house. It covers 6 acres and has 160 rooms, 47 fireplaces, 950 doors, and 10,000 windowpanes. More amazing is the reason for her thirty-eight years of unending work. Sarah Winchester, heiress of the Winchester name and fortune, kept workmen busy for nearly four decades, spending $5 million in an era when a workman earned only 50 cents for a day's labor. And she did all this because a psychic told her the ghosts of people killed by the Winchester Repeating Rifle had cursed her. To escape, she had to move west and start work on a house that was never to be finished. The spiritualist promised as long as

Sarah worked, she would live. Pained by the loss of her husband to tuberculosis and her six-month-old daughter to a childhood disease a few years before, Sarah Winchester invested her life and fortune avoiding death. It didn't work.

We can't avoid death, but we can change our view of it. The teaching of the Bible is that life continues after death. This "life eternal" is a gift of God for those who trust in Him. Francis Bacon said that "men fear death as children fear to go in the dark." Perhaps that's the problem—we think that darkness is on the other side. The apostle Paul said something different: "We are confident, I say, and would prefer to be away from the body and at home with the Lord" (2 Corinthians 5:8 NIV).

Why does one person fear death while another embraces it? Knowledge of God. Such knowledge opens our eyes to see that there is more to life than just this existence; to know that birth is a beginning and so is death. What really counts in life is connecting to the One who gives life, both physical and eternal. John Milton understood what was important when he said, "Death is the golden key that opens the palace of eternity." Milton called it a palace; Jesus called it a mansion custom-built by the Great Carpenter Himself. That puts a new perspective on an old fear—one we can live with and die with.

Life
Life After Life

What Matters Most...

- ◎ Looking beyond the grave and remembering that Christ has made eternal life possible.

- ◎ Living this day to its fullest and not worrying about your last day.

- ◎ Knowing your last day on earth can be your first day in heaven.

- ◎ Remembering that even Jesus died and that His death changed death for every believer.

- ◎ Living life so that you collect treasures in heaven and build a worthwhile memory on earth.

What Doesn't Matter...

- ◎ Fearing the inevitable. Fear is normal but should never control your life. Dread is crippling and a waste of the life you have.

- ◎ Worrying about the time of your departure—there is so much life in the "right now." There is no sin in feeling good.

- ◎ Being so earthly minded that you are no heavenly good. Live every moment for the gift that it is, knowing that God is the giver of life. Don't lose sight of Him.

- ◎ Feeling that life is unfair. It often is. Happiness comes from recognizing the challenges of life and facing them head-on.

Focus Points...

The last enemy that will be abolished is death.
1 CORINTHIANS 15:26 NASB

Because God's children are human beings—made of flesh and blood—Jesus also became flesh and blood by being born in human form. For only as a human being could he die, and only by dying could he break the power of the Devil, who had the power of death. Only in this way could he deliver those who have lived all their lives as slaves to the fear of dying.
HEBREWS 2:14–15 NLT

He has made all of this plain to us by the coming of Christ Jesus, our Savior, who broke the power of death and showed us the way to everlasting life through the Good News.
2 TIMOTHY 1:10 NLT

**what
really
counts**

Now we know that if the earthly tent we live in is destroyed, we have a building from God, an eternal house in heaven, not built by human hands.
2 CORINTHIANS 5:1 NIV

Here is a test to see if your mission on earth is finished. If you are alive, it isn't.

FRANCIS BACON

Through life's valley be a vale of tears, a brighter scene beyond that vale appears.

WILLIAM COWPER

Life
The Day You Live

> The thief comes only to steal and kill
> and destroy; I came that they may
> have life, and have it abundantly.
> JOHN 10:10 NASB

what really counts

When Theodore Roosevelt was president he was traveling in a horse-drawn trolley. With him was his good friend Secret Service agent "Big" Bill Craig. The driver lost control of the trolley and it crashed, throwing everyone onboard to the ground. President Roosevelt was injured but would recover; "Big" Bill Craig died at the scene. Today every American has heard of Teddy Roosevelt, but very few know of Bill Craig. Does this mean that in the end Roosevelt was a success and Craig a failure? If President Roosevelt were alive today, he would tell us otherwise.

When do you begin to live? At conception? Certainly that is true physically, but what about the other facets of your life? When do they come alive? When do you really begin to live the life you were meant to live? Philosophers have written thousands of pages of difficult-to-follow text, but the answer is much simpler than that. You begin to live when you discover your personal purpose. In an age of cookie-cutter people, there is a powerful urge to conform. It's natural. It's to be expected. It can also be detrimental. One of the most important things in life is knowing who you are and what you are meant to do.

The apostle Paul was a colorful, outspoken dynamo who went from persecuting the first-century church to being its greatest spokesman. Today we read the Bible and envision him as a mighty orator, gripping his listeners with powerful rhetoric—a first-century Billy Graham or Charles Spurgeon. Paul's view of himself was very different. He saw himself as a bumbling, stuttering, weak, unimpressive representative of Christ. Yet he changed the world. Why? Because he knew his purpose was to spread the gospel, and that was all that mattered to him. Everything else took a backseat.

The purpose of life is to have a life of godly purpose. This isn't always easy to discover or implement. Sometimes it takes years to learn what you are made to do. There are so many distractions to sidetrack you. An old Christian document from the seventeenth century, the Shorter Catechism, reads, "The chief end of man is to glorify God and enjoy Him forever." That's what's important. That's when you begin to live. When you find your purpose and live it to God's glory, then you are truly alive.

LIFE

Life
The Day You Live

What Matters Most...

- Living with a purpose. Renew or discover your godly purpose if you have one; discover one if you do not.

- Living beyond yourself. Life is meant to be shared with others. The returns are great.

- Living in two directions. When you interact with others you are living life in the horizontal. When you relate to God, you are living in the vertical.

- Reflecting heaven on earth. The closer you are to God, the more you live with His power.

- Forging a legacy that lives after your death.

What Doesn't Matter...

- Building wealth. There is no sin or shame in acquiring wealth, but it will always be your actions that will be remembered.

- Acquiring fame. Fame seldom reflects a person's true nature.

- Success at the expense of others.

- Being first. Being noble is better.

- The opinion of many at the expense of God.

Focus Points...

The LORD God formed man of dust from the ground, and breathed into his nostrils the breath of life; and man became a living being.
GENESIS 2:7 NASB

I tell you, do not worry about your life, what you will eat or drink; or about your body, what you will wear. Is not life more important than food, and the body more important than clothes?
MATTHEW 6:25 NIV

Choose to love the LORD your God and to obey him and commit yourself to him, for he is your life. Then you will live long in the land the LORD swore to give your ancestors Abraham, Isaac, and Jacob.
DEUTERONOMY 30:20 NLT

what really counts

If we live, we live to the Lord; and if we die, we die to the Lord. Therefore, whether we live or die, we are the Lord's.
ROMANS 14:8 NKJV

Life is not a holiday, but an education. And the one eternal lesson for us all is how better we can love.
HENRY DRUMMOND

Life can only be understood backwards, but it must be lived forwards.
SÖREN KIERKEGAARD

What Matters Most to Me About
Life

Death is the period at the end of one existence, but it is also the first word of the next life. To ponder death is to ponder life; to consider life is to acknowledge death. Spend some time considering the following:

◉ *Fix your position. Every journey has a destination, but no trip can be taken unless you first know where you are. When making a road trip to Miami, it's important to know if you're starting from San Diego or New York. Life is no different. Jot down a few words that describe where you are in life.*

_____

_____

_____

_____

_____

◉ *Chart a course. Direction comes from destination. Once you know where you are, then you can plot a course to where you need to be. This takes some soul-searching, but an honest appraisal of purpose and heart's desire will help determine where you want to be. Comment about where you would like your life to be.*

_____

_____

_____

_____

_____

_____

◎ *Take inventory. A wise traveler first determines what is at hand, what should be acquired, what should be taken, and what should be left behind. What really counts to you? What should matter? Jot down the things of real value, and don't forget the spiritual.*

_____

_____

_____

_____

_____

_____

_____

_____

◎ *Enjoy the trip. We get only one life, and although it can be challenging and hard, it can also be enjoyable. Learn to look in the unexpected places.*

_____

_____

_____

_____

_____

_____

_____

LORD, remind me how brief my time on earth will be. Remind me that my days are numbered, and that my life is fleeing away.
PSALM 39:4 NLT

LIFE

GOD

An Introduction

> God is spirit, and those who worship Him must worship in spirit and truth.
>
> JOHN 4:24 NASB

what really counts

S. F. B. Morse, inventor of the telegraph, sent the first message over the miles between Washington, D.C., and Baltimore, Maryland. On May 24, 1844, he sent a message that not only proved his telegraph worked but also revealed the heart of the man: "What hath God wrought." He was not alone in such sentiments. On Christmas Eve 1968, William Anders, Jim Lovell, and Frank Borman read from the Genesis 1 creation account in a live broadcast from *Apollo 8* as it orbited the moon 240,000 miles away. With darkness of space around them and the bleak, gray soil of the moon below, their thoughts ran to earth, their home, and the God who created it all.

God

God Is Thinking of You

> You, Lord, are good, and ready to forgive, and abundant in lovingkindness to all who call upon You.
>
> PSALM 86:5 NASB

Auguste Rodin is best remembered for his bronze sculpture *The Thinker*. It shows a man seated, hunched over, head resting on his hand, deep in thought. We are interested in what people think. "A penny for your thoughts" has probably rolled off your lips from time to time. Have you ever wondered what God thinks about? He who knows all things, comprehends every fact, every detail, knows the operation of the universe from its tiniest particle to its largest galaxy; what occupies His mind? The answer is as simple as it is surprising: He thinks about you. He thinks about me.

We tend to think of ourselves as insignificant. After all, there are six billion other people on this planet. Faced with a number like that, it is normal to wonder if we matter much at all. But we do. There may be billions who don't know our names, but the One who really counts, does. Jesus taught that God knows every time a sparrow falls and went on to say that

The human mind naturally thinks of God. And why wouldn't it? God is the Creator of all that we see and all that we are. We are linked to Him by an umbilical that reaches from our world to His heaven. We are the children of His creation and through Christ are the children of His heart. God is small enough to fit the heart and big enough to fill the universe. We were meant to fit God, and He designed us so that He would fit us. It is easy to fall into the trap of thinking that God is "out there" when in reality He is right here. There is no physical distance between us and our Creator. He is no more than a whispered prayer away.

Nobody seriously believes the universe was made by God without being persuaded that He takes care of His works.

JOHN CALVIN

we are far more important than sparrows. He then added that God has the hairs of the head numbered. It's an ancient way of saying that something as common and as small as a hair matters.

God thinks of you. It's a stunning thought. It's nice to be remembered by a friend, to receive a card in the mail or an unexpected gift, but to understand that the Creator of the universe has us on His mind is soul shaking. And it should be. You see, we should be thinking about God too. He should be at the forefront of our thoughts.

Can we matter that much to God? The Princeton University astronomer Henry Norris Russell gave a lecture about the Milky Way galaxy—our galaxy. Afterward, a woman asked, "If our world is so little, and the universe is so great, can we believe that God pays any attention to us?" "That depends," Russell said, "on how big a God you believe in." What really counts in life is knowing that God is big enough to know you—no matter how little you feel. And knowing that fills us with a sense of meaning and value. Every time you look at your watch, or pause from your labors, take a moment to remember that God is thinking about you—by name. It's that personal.

God
God Is Thinking of You

What Matters Most...

- There is a God. This truth has been debated for generations, but the bottom line remains the same. God was; God is; God will forever be.

- God is close. He is not confined to the pages of the Bible or the walls of a church. He is close to you right now.

- God is not obscure to you. Finding God is easy because He has already found you. The more you open up to Him, the more clearly you see.

- You are not obscure to God. You may go through life unnoticed or with great fame, but either way, God is aware of you and of every detail of your life.

- The Maker of heaven and earth is thinking about you. In that knowledge is freedom and strength.

What Doesn't Matter...

- Earthly significance. The sheer number of people in the world can make you feel small and unimportant. God doesn't look at the mob, but the person in the mob.

- Social status. While most people are impressed with fame and fortune, God is not so moved. He cares about the person, not the trappings.

- Background. Experience, lineage, gender, and race matter more to people than to God. God doesn't look on the outward appearance of a person, but at the heart.

- Denial. God thinks of you even if you don't think of Him. It's tragic to live in disbelief, but no matter what you think, God is there and aware of every individual.

Focus Points...

God is faithful, through whom you were called into fellowship with His Son, Jesus Christ our Lord.
1 Corinthians 1:9 NASB

I have called you back from the ends of the earth so you can serve me. For I have chosen you and will not throw you away.
Isaiah 41:9 NLT

If you, then, though you are evil, know how to give good gifts to your children, how much more will your Father in heaven give good gifts to those who ask him!
Matthew 7:11–12 NIV

They shall be My people, and I will be their God.
Jeremiah 32:38 NKJV

The very hairs on your head are all numbered. So don't be afraid; you are more valuable to him than a whole flock of sparrows.
Matthew 10:30–31 NLT

what really counts

The relationship between God and a man is more private and intimate than any possible relation between two fellow creatures.

C. S. Lewis

Best of all, God is with us.

John Wesley

29

God
God Has a Plan

A man's ways are in full view of the LORD, and he examines all his paths.

PROVERBS 5:21 NIV

what really counts

Charles Haddon Spurgeon is considered one of the greatest preachers to have ever lived. He was a celebrity in his day. Newspapers printed his Sunday sermons so those who couldn't make it to church could at least read what he said. One day a young theology student came to Spurgeon deeply upset that he couldn't understand certain passages of the Bible. Spurgeon gave a short response: "Give the Lord credit for knowing things you don't understand."

God has a plan. In His mind, it is clear and detailed. Some of that plan He has revealed to us through the Bible. Do we know it all? No, we don't. It's doubtful that we are capable of understanding the details and nuances. But we know enough, and what we know tells us that God is not haphazard. The more we know about science—the complexities of biology, the structure of chemistry, the intricacies of the universe—the more we see that God is a Designer. The universe operates according to a set of laws written by God. What we see is not the end result of happenstance and chance, but of a well-designed plan.

God's plans extend beyond the laws of physics. He has a plan for His people. That includes you. If you are honest with yourself, it sometimes appears that there is more chaos than order, more confusion than direction. Humans have been going into space since the Russian Yury Gagarin became the first human in orbit on April 12, 1961. Since then, tens of thousands of photos of earth have been taken, and each one gives a wider perspective of the world. It's normal to think that our view is the only view, but God sees so much more and is working in more ways than we can imagine. His view includes not only the present, but the past and the future; not only our spot on the planet, but the whole world and heaven, too.

Planning is a part of life. It is a good and holy thing to do. When we give thought to who we are and what we should do with the gift of our lives, we are imitating the One who created us. We should plan our lives, and we should include God in those plans. When we do, we will better understand that God has included us in His plans. The keys to knowing God's plan are prayer, worship, and Bible study.

God
God Has a Plan

What Matters Most...

◎ Knowing that God can plan. He's not an impersonal, cosmic force; He's a thinking Being who can formulate a plan.

◎ Knowing that God has planned. The Bible reminds you repeatedly that God forged His plan before the universe began. Life is not an accident.

◎ Knowing that He has a personal plan for you. God works with nations, but He loves the individual. Christ's coming, ministry, death, and resurrection were planned with you in mind.

◎ Knowing that His plan is forever. You know what it is like to have your plans changed by the unexpected. Nothing can alter or thwart God's plan.

What Doesn't Matter...

◎ Attempting to change God's plans. Some want to rewrite God's work but have never succeeded. What He has planned will come about.

◎ Second-guessing God. He has the larger perspective and timeless experience. He knows better than you do.

◎ Knowing every detail. It's doubtful the human mind could hold all the details of God's plan. Learning as much as possible is important but no human knows it all.

Focus Points...

Our God is in the heavens; He does whatever He pleases.
PSALM 115:3 NASB

The LORD does whatever pleases him throughout all heaven and earth, and on the seas and in their depths.
PSALM 135:6 NLT

I make known the end from the beginning, from ancient times, what is still to come. I say: My purpose will stand, and I will do all that I please.
ISAIAH 46:10 NIV

In Him also we have obtained an inheritance, being pre-destined according to the purpose of Him who works all things according to the counsel of His will, that we who first trusted in Christ should be to the praise of His glory.
EPHESIANS 1:11–12 NKJV

what really counts

[Abraham] was absolutely convinced that God was able to do anything he promised.
ROMANS 4:21 NLT

The only possible answer to the destiny of man is to seek without respite to fulfill God's purpose.

PAUL TOURNIER

God loves us the way we are, but too much to leave us that way.

LEIGHTON FORD

33

God
Remembering God

When I remember You on my bed, I meditate on You in the night watches. Because You have been my help, therefore in the shadow of Your wings I will rejoice.

PSALM 63:6–7 NKJV

what really counts

New Year's Day and Halloween have something in common. They are a couple of the few holidays we celebrate that have nothing to do with remembering. Most holidays are set aside to jog our memories. Christmas, Good Friday, and Easter cause us to recall the birth, death, and resurrection of Christ. Presidents' Day, Independence Day, Labor Day, Memorial Day, and Veterans Day revolve around the act of remembering. Remembering is important.

God may be the most forgotten person in the world. For those involved in church, those who make their way to worship services each week, thoughts of God are common, but for the rest of the world, God remains forgotten until needed. There is irony in all this. God's fingerprints are everywhere. Whether we look at the night sky or study the machinery of the human cell, we see design, the clear evidence of the Designer. But there is other evidence: the quiet sensation of

34

God's presence felt in our minds and hearts. God seldom shouts, but He does make Himself known in a thousand quiet ways.

Studies done for the Office of Naval Research by Dr. George Miller indicate that most of us can accurately remember only seven items from any list read to us. Some have suggested that this is why the number seven occurs so much in human history: the Seven Wonders of the World, seven basic notes on the music scale, seven deadly sins, seven ages of man, and the seven seas. Our memories are finite and often faulty, but they are still powerful tools for life.

Memory is a tricky thing, and with finite brains we can remember only so much. That makes it all the more important to remember God—daily and not as an afterthought. Hundreds of images from television, messages from radio, and basic events of life assault our minds. In the midst of all that is the opportunity to remember the eternal God, and by so doing, encounter Him in a way that changes our lives. We remember God because He is worth remembering and because of what it allows us to become. Choosing to remember God is choosing to remember that we have a greater purpose and are part of a greater plan. God in the brain is God in the heart, and God in the heart is God in the soul. In everything and in every day, remember your God.

God
Remembering God

What Matters Most...

- Learning that memory has a purpose. Memory is not an accident; it is part of God's design. You have memory for many reasons, including the joy of remembering God.

- The more you know of God, the more there is to remember. And the more you remember of God and His ways, the better equipped you are to face life in all its fullness.

- Remembering brings courage. By recalling how good God *has been,* the better able you are to find courage in knowing how good God *is.*

- Remembering God is a reminder that you are never alone. Such remembrance warms the heart and strengthens the resolve.

What Doesn't Matter...

- Anything that seems more important than your Creator. There are thousands of good and noble things worthy of your attention, but nothing eclipses the glory and purpose of God.

- The ability to remember everything. Some people have better memories than others, but no one can recall every detail of life; therefore, you must remind yourself what is important.

- The flashes and glitter of life can pull your eyes away from God. While there is nothing wrong with flash and glitter, it pales in importance to knowing God.

- The negative. The human mind tends to remember the bad over the good.

Focus Points...

I shall remember the deeds of the LORD; surely I will remember Your wonders of old. I will meditate on all Your work and muse on Your deeds.
PSALM 77:11–12 NASB

I remember your ancient laws, O LORD, and I find comfort in them.
PSALM 119:52 NIV

Don't let the excitement of youth cause you to forget your Creator. Honor him in your youth before you grow old and no longer enjoy living.
ECCLESIASTES 12:1 NLT

When my soul fainted within me, I remembered the LORD; and my prayer went up to You, into Your holy temple.
JONAH 2:7 NKJV

what really counts

Think of the wonderful works he has done, the miracles, and the judgments he handed down.
1 CHRONICLES 16:12 NLT

This is the creator: By his love, our Father; by his power, our Lord; by his wisdom, our maker and designer.
SAINT IRENAEUS

I have never been able to conceive mankind without him [God].
FYODOR DOSTOYEVSKY

37

God
The Everyday God

The LORD looks down from heaven and sees the whole human race. From his throne he observes all who live on the earth. He made their hearts, so he understands everything they do.

PSALM 33:13–15 NLT

what really counts

We remember King Solomon for his God-given wisdom, but we also remember the Jewish king for building the first temple. It was an amazing structure, not because of its size but because of the great craftsmanship and cost that went into its construction. It took seven years to build, and was constructed of only the finest material. Everything inside the temple was plated with gold: walls, ceilings, furnishings, everything. Only the finest woods were used; only the best sculptors were retained. They called it the "House of God," and people of the day believed that God would dwell there.

Despite its cost and beauty, Solomon knew that no building could hold God. Solomon said, "Behold, heaven and the highest heaven cannot contain You, how much less this house which I have built!" (1 Kings 8:27 NASB). Solomon was right. No single building, no complex of structures, could begin to hold the infinite God. And not only is He not bound by buildings, He is not bound by time. We often call Sunday the Lord's Day. There is nothing wrong with that as long as we remember that Monday through Saturday are also His days. God is an everyday God. Christians are not Christians on Sunday only, but every day of their lives.

It's hard to grasp a concept like omnipresence—the attribute of God that teaches He is everywhere present at all times, that there is no place on earth or in heaven where God is not. Bedrooms and boardrooms, indoors and outdoors, stadiums and shacks, God is there. And not just as an impersonal force, but as a living, loving, active being.

God is in the church building you see as you drive to work, but He is not *just* there; He is also at your destination, in your home, around the corner, and in the backseat. God is in the heart of that believing friend you have, but He is also in the heart of the believing stranger. The temple Solomon built would later be destroyed by an invading army. Was God destroyed with the temple? Of course not. No one believed that He was. They knew what we need to know: that God does not live in buildings but lives in people; that He isn't confined to Sundays but works in our lives every day of the week. Knowing that counts; believing that really counts.

God
The Everyday God

What Matters Most...

◎ Seeing God as close rather than as distant. He is less than a whisper away, closer than anyone can imagine. He is not confined by space.

◎ Seeing God on Monday. And every other day of the week. He is unconfined by time. Faith works out seven days a week.

◎ Experiencing God. He is more than the subject of theology books. He is the One your life orbits around. Knowing is good; experiencing is better.

◎ Letting God be big enough to fill the universe. He doesn't need your permission, but you need to expand your thinking.

What Doesn't Matter...

◎ The how. It's natural to wonder how God is everywhere at the same time, but no theory or math formula will be able to describe the truth of it. Nonetheless, it remains true.

◎ The numbers. No one can provide a gallon of love or twenty feet of hope. God is beyond measurement, but He is not beyond your experience.

◎ The abstract. So often one speaks of God as the subject of a debate and loses Him as a person. The nature of God is meant to create a relationship, not a debate. Knowing God is more important than knowing about Him.

Focus Points...

To you it was shown that you might know that the LORD, He is God; there is no other besides Him.

DEUTERONOMY 4:35 NASB

No temptation has seized you except what is common to man. And God is faithful; he will not let you be tempted beyond what you can bear. But when you are tempted, he will also provide a way out so that you can stand up under it.

1 CORINTHIANS 10:13 NIV

Before the mountains were brought forth, or ever You had formed the earth and the world, even from everlasting to everlasting, You are God.

PSALM 90:2 NKJV

what really counts

Whatever is good and perfect comes to us from God above, who created all heaven's lights. Unlike them, he never changes or casts shifting shadows.

JAMES 1:17 NLT

God does not give us everything we want, but He does fulfill all His promises ... leading us along the best and straightest paths to Himself.

DIETRICH BONHOEFFER

God is the Best and Most Orderly Workman of all.

COPERNICUS

What Matters Most to Me About
God

God wants to be known by you and has revealed Himself in creation and in His Bible. He has also equipped you with the ability to experience Him. To know Him better, think about the following:

◎ *Look for God's fingerprints. The universe is filled with proof of God's existence and His intelligent life. All it takes is a willingness to open your eyes and look. Make note of a few ways in which you see God in creation.*

_____

_____

_____

_____

_____

_____

_____

what
really
counts

◎ *Look on the inside. While it is fascinating to see what God has done "out there," it is equally thrilling to see what He is doing inside you. In what ways has God made Himself known to you? Write down a few occurrences.*

_____

_____

_____

_____

_____

_____

_____

◉ *Look at others. You probably know someone who is a deeply committed Christian. Write down a few things you've seen in his or her life that makes that person different.*

_____

_____

_____

_____

_____

_____

_____

_____

_____

◉ *The Bible is God's written revelation. Read Genesis 1 and John 1 and ask yourself, "What is the writer saying about God?" Jot down your observations.*

_____

_____

_____

_____

_____

_____

_____

_____

_____

God saw everything that He had made, and indeed it was very good.
GENESIS 1:31 NKJV

JESUS

An Introduction

> You know the grace of our Lord Jesus Christ, that though He was rich, yet for your sake He became poor, so that you through His poverty might become rich.
>
> 2 CORINTHIANS 8:9 NASB

what really counts

There is no other person more widely known than Jesus. Even our calendars mark His life with the letters AD—*anno domini*—"in the year of the Lord." He is the most popular subject of artists, poets, and writers. More books have been written about Him than any other person ever to live. John Newton wrote, "How sweet the name of Jesus sounds in a believer's ear!" The name of Jesus also sounds sweet in the hearts and minds of believers around the world and throughout time.

Jesus is not only a historical character, but He is also a contemporary Savior. Jesus is not a past-tense person; He is a present-tense reality. We celebrate His birth, His death, and His resurrection. Churches meet on Sundays because that was the day Christ rose from the grave. Jesus left His stamp on humankind in general and on the individual specifically. Kings did not intimidate Him; the poor did not offend Him; the sick did not discuss Him. "I came to seek and to save that which is lost," He said. He had all of us in mind when He said it. He had you in mind. Jesus was the Perfect, living and dying for the imperfect.

The simple truth is, Jesus cannot be ignored, cannot be confined to the pages of history, and will not surrender His love for us. He touches and changes lives. Jesus is like us, for us, and with us. Knowing that really matters.

> If ever man was God or God man, Jesus Christ was both.
>
> LORD BYRON

Jesus

Jesus—Like Us

> Because he himself suffered when he was tempted, he is able to help those who are being tempted.
>
> HEBREWS 2:18 NIV

No greater paradox exists than the person of Jesus Christ. Saint Gregory of Nazianzus summed it up when, in AD 381, he wrote, "He began His ministry by being hungry, yet He is the Bread of Life. Jesus ended His earthly ministry by being thirsty, yet He is the Living Water. Jesus was weary, yet He is our rest. Jesus paid tribute, yet He is the King. Jesus was accused of having a demon, yet He cast out demons. Jesus wept, yet He wipes away our tears. Jesus was sold for thirty pieces of silver, yet He redeemed the world. Jesus was brought as a lamb to the slaughter, yet He is the Good Shepherd. Jesus died, yet by His death He destroyed the power of death."

For some, Christianity is all about trying to be like Jesus. A more important truth is how much Jesus became like us. Certainly He is sinless; and yes, He is God in the flesh, but Jesus took on the same form—our form. He entered this world as a baby. Why? Because that's how we come into this

what really counts

world. He went through childhood and adolescence. Why? Because we do. He worked for a living until He began His public ministry; He felt hunger and thirst, weariness and rest, joy and sadness. He experienced rejection, suffered from cruel and untrue accusations; He faced temptation; He was misunderstood; He died. Why? Because we do. He was also resurrected and lives forever. Why? Because we will.

No discussion about what is important in life is complete without understanding that Jesus became like us. The temptation is to think of Jesus as the used-to-be Savior, the guy from history who lived so long ago and walked around the small country of His birth, but it is a world-class mistake to limit Jesus to those years. Jesus is a now Savior, a twenty-first-century solution to the challenges of this life and the next. Each day we should remind ourselves that not only did Jesus like us, He *became* like us. We have a Savior who not only relates to us but to whom we can relate. He not only knows what we face in life, He *understands*. It was love that compelled Jesus to take on human form and experience life as we do. Not because He didn't understand—He did—but so that we can understand. We can relate to a Savior who knows hunger, weariness, rejection, and more.

Jesus
Jesus—Like Us

What Matters Most...

◎ Jesus became like you. God in the flesh. Hard to imagine but very true. It's good to know that you have a Savior who knows what this life is like.

◎ Jesus came for you. Knowing that Jesus came on purpose and with purpose matters. He didn't come on a lark but to achieve your salvation.

◎ Jesus understands what this life is like. Since Jesus endured the hardships of this life, you can know that you have an understanding Savior and not a judgmental one.

◎ Moving from head knowledge to heart knowledge. This is nothing more than trivia if you don't connect with Christ personally. Make the effort. He did.

What **Doesn't** Matter...

◎ Centuries. Jesus is as real, as alive, as important, and as involved as He ever was. Time doesn't change His love or commitment.

◎ Distance. Jesus conducted His ministry in a small country many miles from where you live. Distance doesn't matter to Jesus. He is and remains the Savior for all believers wherever they are.

◎ Being an outsider. "I came to seek and to save that which is lost," Jesus said. That includes everyone. Jesus didn't come because you are worthy but because you need someone who was worthy.

Focus Points...

The Word became flesh, and dwelt among us, and we saw His glory, glory as of the only begotten from the Father, full of grace and truth.
JOHN 1:14 NASB

When the time had fully come, God sent his Son, born of a woman, born under law, to redeem those under law, that we might receive the full rights of sons.
GALATIANS 4:4–5 NIV

Let this mind be in you which was also in Christ Jesus, who, being in the form of God, did not consider it robbery to be equal with God, but made Himself of no reputation, taking the form of a bondservant, and coming in the likeness of men.
PHILIPPIANS 2:5–7 NKJV

what really counts

Without controversy great is the mystery of godliness: God was manifest in the flesh, justified in the Spirit, seen of angels, preached unto the Gentiles, believed on in the world, received up into glory.
1 TIMOTHY 3:16 KJV

He came in complete human form to meet a universal need in a way that is adequate for all times and places and is without parallel or substitute.

H. D. LEWIS

Nothing shall detract from the figure of Christ!

LEONARDO DA VINCI

Jesus

Jesus—For Us

> There is one God and one mediator between God and men, the man Christ Jesus, who gave himself as a ransom for all men—the testimony given in its proper time.
>
> 1 Timothy 2:5–6 NIV

what really counts

The world-famous architect Frank Lloyd Wright would not confine himself to just designing a home; he'd also design all the furniture that went into the home. Most people thought he was a great architect, but his furniture left something to be desired. The pieces looked wonderful but were uncomfortable. Good-looking furniture is nice, but most of us want our furnishings to be functional. Fashions and people change. Empires that seemed strong, invincible, and certain to stand until the end of time have slipped into the pages of the history books. Rome, Greece, and other great nations fell only to be replaced by other nations. It seems that great things sooner or later melt into the past tense.

Jesus, however, is past, present, and future. It's a strange description to use in relation to a person, but it's a good term. Jesus is not a has-been. He is as active today as He was when He strolled the dusty streets of Galilee. But we might want to ask, "What is He doing now?" Now, as He was then, Jesus is focused on us, the ones for whom He came, taught, suffered, died, and was resurrected. That part of Christ's ministry is over, but His work continues—Jesus works for us.

Reading through the New Testament shows that Jesus still has us at the center of His attention. Today and every day, Jesus intercedes on behalf of believers. That simply means Jesus stands before God and speaks on our behalf. He stands sinless for the sinful and bridges the gap between God and us. He is also involved in helping believers. Life can be difficult, but it never needs to be lived alone. Some view Jesus as a candy dispenser, dolling out solutions to problems whenever we put in the right change. Jesus doesn't solve all our problems, but He empowers us to do so. He is also listening. In a world that prides itself on talk, Jesus remains the faithful listener; He turns away no one who comes to Him. He is also constructing a place for believers. He said, "When everything is ready, I will come and get you, so that you will always be with me where I am" (John 14:3 NLT). We don't know the nature of the construction, but we do know its purpose is to keep us close to Him.

The list is huge, but the idea is clear: Jesus is for us. He lived for us; He died for us; He rose from the dead for us; He ascended into heaven for us; and He continues to love us. The world needs that kind of attention. We need that kind of attention. You need it too. The key is to see Jesus as more than Someone who was and did, but also as Someone who is and does.

Jesus
Jesus—For Us

What Matters Most...

◎ Remembering that Jesus isn't done. His physical work on earth is finished, but His work in heaven continues. He works on your behalf.

◎ Believing that Jesus stands in the gap. Sin separates humanity from God; Jesus bridges that chasm. Without Him you are lost; with Him you have life.

◎ Jesus speaks for you. Jesus stands before God and speaks on your behalf. He is your Mediator and the only One who can do that work.

◎ Jesus lived and died and lives—all for us. We were the focus of His attention; we were His goal—we still are.

What **Doesn't** Matter...

◎ Feeling adrift. You no longer sail the seas of life alone. Your past may make you feel guilty and outside of God's love. Jesus puts you back in the center.

◎ Feeling alone. Jesus has never turned His back on anyone who came to Him in faith. There's no reason to believe He ever will.

◎ Feeling left out. In a world of "us" and "them," it's good to know that Jesus doesn't discriminate. Anyone with belief can come to Him and find a listening Savior.

◎ Feeling unworthy. Most people feel unworthy of Christ's love. That is true, but it doesn't matter. Salvation isn't based on your worthiness but on Jesus' worthiness.

Focus Points...

I am the good shepherd; the good shepherd lays down His life for the sheep ... I am the good shepherd, and I know My own and My own know Me.
JOHN 10:11, 14 NASB

He has rescued us from the dominion of darkness and brought us into the kingdom of the Son he loves, in whom we have redemption, the forgiveness of sins.
COLOSSIANS 1:13–14 NIV

My dear children, I am writing this to you so that you will not sin. But if you do sin, there is someone to plead for you before the Father. He is Jesus Christ, the one who pleases God completely. He is the sacrifice for our sins. He takes away not only our sins but the sins of all the world.
1 JOHN 2:1–2 NLT

what really counts

Who then will condemn us? Will Christ Jesus? No, for he is the one who died for us and was raised to life for us and is sitting at the place of highest honor next to God, pleading for us.
ROMANS 8:34 NLT

Jesus was God and man in one person, that God and man might be happy together again.

GEORGE WHITEFIELD

He is the greatest influence in the world today. There is . . . a fifth Gospel being written—the work of Jesus Christ in the hearts and lives of men and nations.

W. H. GRIFFITH THOMAS

Jesus
Jesus—With Us

> Where two or three have gathered together in My name, I am there in their midst.
>
> MATTHEW 18:20 NASB

When the *Apollo 11* mission landed two men on the moon on July 20, 1969, then President Richard Nixon exclaimed, "This is the greatest day since creation!" The evangelist Billy Graham was with him and gently reminded the president of the Resurrection. No matter how great a historical event, nothing will ever obscure the Resurrection. While there are many qualities and achievements that separate Jesus from other famous historical characters, the Resurrection seals the deal. Jesus not only *was* but He *is*—and will continue to be forever.

Philip Yancey wrote in his book *The Jesus I Never Knew*, "You can gauge the size of a ship that has passed out of sight by the huge wake it leaves behind." Jesus left a historical and spiritual wake that continues to roll across the surface of humanity. Lives were changed in His day; lives are changed today. The passing of time has not changed Christ, not diminished His impact, not dulled His truth, and not passed Him into oblivion. Every day hundreds of people encounter Christ, and their lives are forever changed. Jesus walked the earth for forty days after His resurrection. In some of His last words to the disciples, He said, "Surely I am with you always, to the very end of the age." The word He used for *age* means "forevermore." Jesus is the "forevermore" Savior.

It is one thing to admire a great historical leader, but it is another to commit your life to someone who lived two millennia before. With Jesus, we place our faith in Someone who did indeed live two thousand years ago but who continues to live today. Jesus promised to be with His disciples to the end of the age, and it is a promise transferred to every disciple since. And anyone who follows Christ is a disciple.

What really counts in life? Knowing Jesus has not disappeared from the world scene. He can be as real to you today as He was to Peter, James, John, and thousands of others who encountered Him during His earthly ministry. When doctors are able to restore hearing to a deaf person, that person must learn to distinguish sounds. The sounds are there, but learning the difference between a trumpet and a trombone takes some practice. Encountering Jesus where you live takes awareness and practice, but it is an effort that pays throughout eternity.

Jesus
Jesus—With Us

What Matters Most...

◎ Living as if Jesus is alive—because He is. There have been many wise men in history and many famous teachers, but only Jesus defeated death and the grave.

◎ Living as if Jesus is living with you—because He is. Jesus promised to be in the midst of believers. He is in the church during worship, and He is in the heart of the believer.

◎ Living as if there is a tomorrow. Hopelessness plagues many, but it needn't. Jesus promised hope in difficulty and an endless number of tomorrows through faith in Him.

◎ Living as if Christ has made a difference in your life. Let others see what Jesus can do. See what Jesus has done in others.

What Doesn't Matter...

◎ Pretending you don't need others. Everyone needs someone, and everyone needs Jesus.

◎ Terminal thinking—the idea that this is all there is to life, and then come death and the end. Jesus proved there was life after death, and He did so for your benefit.

◎ Living for yourself. Jesus lives for you, and that is an example you should follow. Life is not isolation; life is sharing.

◎ Busyness. Life fills up your hours, but there is always time for Christ. Without Him life is merely a string of good and bad events. With Him life makes sense.

Focus Points...

These things I have spoken to you, so that in Me you may have peace. In the world you have tribulation, but take courage; I have overcome the world.
JOHN 16:33 NASB

Peace I leave with you; my peace I give you. I do not give to you as the world gives. Do not let your hearts be troubled and do not be afraid.
JOHN 14:27 NIV

Don't worry about anything; instead, pray about everything. Tell God what you need, and thank him for all he has done. If you do this, you will experience God's peace, which is far more wonderful than the human mind can understand. His peace will guard your hearts and minds as you live in Christ Jesus.
PHILIPPIANS 4:6–7 NLT

what really counts

Now come I to thee; and these things I speak in the world, that they might have my joy fulfilled in themselves.
JOHN 17:13 KJV

Perhaps the transformation of the disciples of Jesus is the greatest evidence of all for the resurrection.
JOHN SCOTT

Although we have complete salvation through His death, because we are reconciled to God by it, it is by His resurrection, not His death, that we are said to be born to a living hope.

57

JOHN CALVIN

Jesus
Empathy from the Savior

> We do not have a High Priest who cannot sympathize with our weaknesses, but was in all points tempted as we are, yet without sin.
>
> HEBREWS 4:15 NKJV

what really counts

One of the strangest verses in the Bible is Matthew 4:1: "Then Jesus was led by the Spirit into the desert to be tempted by the devil" (NIV). It is strange because of the way it is worded. After Jesus' baptism in the Jordan River, the Holy Spirit led Him into the adjoining wilderness so Satan could tempt Him. Our first response is that Jesus is too important and too pure to have to endure such things. After all, He is God in the flesh, and yet this verse and supporting verses make it clear that it was part of the plan that Jesus begin His ministry by being tempted. Forty days He fasted while exposed to the harsh elements. Satan tempted Him with food, fame, and riches. Jesus resisted every time.

Why bother with all this? Why mention it now? Understanding Christ's temptations helps us understand Christ. There are two words in our language that are similar but distinct. The first is *sympathy*. *Sympathy* is the feeling we have when we feel sorry for someone. A friend receives bad news, and we feel bad for them; we are sympathetic. The word means "to feel for someone." The second word sounds very close, but its meaning is different. *Empathy*, like *sympathy*, refers to a feeling we have for someone else, but the connection is much stronger. *Empathy* means "to feel the same as someone else, to share the same emotion."

Many fathers know what it is like to deliver a baby—they've seen it. They may coach breathing and provide encouraging words. They do the best they can, and they witness the discomfort, the work, and the exhausting emotion. Such fathers can describe in detail everything they saw and experienced. One thing they cannot do is empathize. Only another mother can do that.

Jesus knows what it is like to be tempted. He understands the stresses, the enticements, the felt needs, the longings; He understands this without sinning. When we confess our sins, Jesus not only forgives, He completely understands. That doesn't mean we can be careless; it doesn't mean that we are not responsible. It does mean that when tempted we can go to Jesus in prayer and find Someone who says, "I understand." Knowing that empowers us with greater strength to resist temptation and to overcome difficulty, loneliness, uncertainty, and other pains of life. Whatever you face, take it to Jesus in prayer.

Jesus
Empathy from the Savior

What Matters Most...

◎ Acknowledge temptation. Everyone faces it. Jesus faced it on purpose; you need to face it *with* purpose.

◎ Acknowledge victory in other areas of life. The Bible promises that you never face a situation that you can't overcome by faith.

◎ Acknowledge an understanding Savior. He's been there, so He knows. That's a reminder that your confession is met with understanding.

◎ Acknowledge your particular challenges. Some problems are common to everyone; some are specific to the individual. Choose to face them squarely.

◎ Acknowledge your need for Jesus' help to overcome temptation. He's as happy over your victory as you are.

What Doesn't Matter...

◎ Self-recrimination. Yes, you have private temptation. So does the next person you see. Temptation is not sin; surrendering to it is.

◎ Past failures. Learn from failings, confess the sins, rely on God, and then get on with life.

◎ Future fears. Failures in the past do not mean failures in the future. Victory is possible with Christ.

◎ The opinions others hold of you. It is God's opinion that matters, and He is the God of second chances.

Focus Points...

Come to me, all you who are weary and burdened, and I will give you rest. Take my yoke upon you and learn from me, for I am gentle and humble in heart, and you will find rest for your souls. For my yoke is easy and my burden is light.
MATTHEW 11:28–30 NIV

It was for freedom that Christ set us free; therefore keep standing firm and do not be subject again to a yoke of slavery.
GALATIANS 5:1 NASB

"Come now, and let us reason together," says the LORD, "Though your sins are like scarlet, they shall be as white as snow; though they are red like crimson, they shall be as wool."
ISAIAH 1:18 NKJV

what really counts

He will turn again, he will have compassion upon us; he will subdue our iniquities; and thou wilt cast all their sins into the depths of the sea.
MICAH 7:19 KJV

It is not my ability, but my response to God's ability that counts.

CORRIE TEN BOOM

When trials come your way—as inevitably they will—do not run away. Run to your God and Father.

KAY ARTHUR

What Matters Most to Me About
Jesus

How you see Jesus has an impact on how you see yourself and your faith. Knowing that He is more than a historical character or a good teacher is crucial. Having the "right" Jesus matters.

◉ *Jesus took on human form and all the difficulties that came with that. He did so for everyone. He did so for you. What impact does this have in your life? List a few ways Jesus' coming is important to you.*

_____

_____

_____

_____

_____

_____

_____

_____

◉ *Jesus' work isn't over. He's your Advocate and your Mediator. Jesus bridges the gap between you and God. Jot down a few thoughts about how this has changed your past, changes your present, and will change your future.*

_____

_____

_____

_____

_____

_____

_____

_____

what
really
counts

◎ *The Resurrection proves all of Christ's claims. It happened two thousand years ago, but it still has an impact today. In what ways is the world different because of the Resurrection? In what ways are you different?*

_____

_____

_____

_____

_____

_____

_____

_____

◎ *Jesus is not just sympathetic with your situation; He is empathetic. Having a Savior who not only feels your sorrow but also feels your emotion shows the highest level of love. What does Jesus' empathy teach you about Him? What does it mean to you?*

_____

_____

_____

_____

_____

_____

_____

_____

_____

In His life Christ is an example, showing us how to live; in His death He is a sacrifice, satisfying for our sins; in His resurrection, a conqueror.

MARTIN LUTHER

THE HOLY SPIRIT

An Introduction

> I will ask the Father, and He will give you another Helper, that He may be with you forever; that is the Spirit of truth, whom the world cannot receive, because it does not see Him or know Him, but you know Him because He abides with you and will be in you.
>
> JOHN 14:16–17 NASB

what really counts

For centuries the wind has been harnessed to move boats and ships across the seas. The wind has the power to drive windmills that create electrical energy or even to knock down buildings. The winds of a hurricane or tornado are as destructive as a bomb and can leave little but rubble in their wake. A gentle breeze can keep a child's kite in the air. All of this remains invisible to us. We can see the effects of wind, but never the air itself. We might say the same thing about the Holy Spirit. Often overlooked, little understood, or simply ignored, the Holy Spirit remains a vital part of spiritual life, and yet He is often overlooked.

The Holy Spirit is not a behind-the-scenes actor.

He's out there on the stage of our lives and always has been, but we don't see Him. The Holy Spirit is part of every significant activity of Jesus. He was involved in Jesus' conception, was with Him at His baptism, was with Him in His temptations, was active in His ministry, and much more.

It is no accident that the original New Testament word for spirit is *pneuma* and it means "wind." We use the term today to describe pneumatic tires and tools. *Invisible* doesn't mean nonexistent. The Holy Spirit is active in every area of the believer's life. Like the wind we feel but can't see, so we experience the work of the Holy Spirit without seeing Him. Sometimes, not seeing is believing.

> True discrimination between right and wrong does not then depend on the acuteness of our intelligence, but on the wisdom of the Spirit.
> JOHN CALVIN

The Holy Spirit
Never Alone

> He has identified us as his own by placing the Holy Spirit in our hearts as the first installment of everything he will give us.
>
> 2 CORINTHIANS 1:22 NLT

what really counts

Psychologists say that one of the most powerful fears is abandonment. The thought of having someone close to us leave suddenly is chilling. The disciples knew that feeling. Jesus was clear about His pending death, resurrection, and ascension. Being aware of their unspoken concerns, He said, "I will ask the Father, and He will give you another Helper, that He may be with you forever" (John 14:16 NASB). *Helper* is an interesting word. Sometimes scholars translate the original as "Comforter." The literal rendering of the word means "one called alongside." Jesus was referring to the Holy Spirit. The Holy Spirit is the third person in the Trinity and is certainly the least understood. His name tempts us to think of Him as an "It," but the Holy Spirit is a person who thinks, feels, and makes decisions, just like any other person.

Many verses in the Bible show us that the Holy Spirit lives in the believer and does important work. The way Jesus taught it was this: Jesus would go to the cross, die, be buried and resurrected, and then after a short time He would ascend into heaven. The disciples were nervous about this. After three years of earthly ministry, three years of daily contact with the disciples, He was going to leave their sight. He would not disappear from their lives, but the way He had been relating to them was going to change. The One He called the Holy Spirit would work in their lives.

The Holy Spirit does many things, but one of the most important is this: He is *in* and *with* the believer. When we place our faith in Christ we are never alone. The Comforter, the Helper, the Holy Spirit is there, affirming our place in the kingdom of God as no one else can. Perhaps you've experienced an unexpected inner warmth, a sensation that draws your attention to God as a sense of belonging washes over you. That is the Holy Spirit affirming His presence in you and your place in God's plan. Enjoy it.

New York Times science editor Walter Sullivan wrote a book called *We Are Not Alone,* an investigation into the search for life on other planets. Since then scores of books have been written on the same theme. There is great interest in knowing if intelligent life is "out there." The Bible teaches that there is intelligent life in the life of every believer, and that life has a name: Holy Spirit.

The Holy Spirit
Never Alone

What Matters Most...

◎ Knowing that you do not go through this life alone. The work of the Holy Spirit is close, intimate, and personal. He resides in every person of faith.

◎ Remembering that Jesus called the Holy Spirit "the Comforter." The original word was *paraclete,* which means "one called alongside to help."

◎ Relating to God with the help of the Holy Spirit. The Holy Spirit helps you in your prayer, in your worship, and in your awareness of God.

◎ Opening yourself to His leadership. Those times when you've lacked peace about a decision may have been a warning from the Spirit.

What Doesn't Matter...

◎ The belief that you have to do it "on your own." You were meant to live your life, run your business, and start your family with the help of God.

◎ Full understanding. The relationship between God the Father, God the Son, and God the Holy Spirit is impossible to describe fully, but it is nonetheless true.

◎ Denominations. Some denominations emphasize the Holy Spirit more than others, but He is not confined to a particular group.

Focus Points...

When the Counselor comes, whom I will send to you from the Father, the Spirit of truth who goes out from the Father, he will testify about me.
JOHN 15:26 NIV

The Helper, the Holy Spirit, whom the Father will send in My name, He will teach you all things, and bring to your remembrance all that I said to you.
JOHN 14:26 NASB

People who aren't Christians can't understand these truths from God's Spirit. It all sounds foolish to them because only those who have the Spirit can understand what the Spirit means.
1 CORINTHIANS 2:14 NLT

what really counts

In Him you also trusted, after you heard the word of truth, the gospel of your salvation; in whom also, having believed, you were sealed with the Holy Spirit of promise.
EPHESIANS 1:13 NKJV

God works immediately by His Spirit in and on the wills of His saints.

JOHN OWEN

If we recognize the Spirit of God as the unique fountain of truth, we shall never despise the truth wherever it may appear, unless we wish to do dishonor to the Spirit of God.
JOHN CALVIN

The Holy Spirit
Personal Fire Alarm

> When he comes, he will convince the
> world of its sin, and of God's righteous-
> ness, and of the coming judgment.
>
> JOHN 16:8 NLT

what really counts

Most states require new homes to be equipped with fire alarms. Such alarms are easy to overlook, and they demand little attention—until they go off. Their squeal pierces to the bone and is able to wake the soundest sleeper. Unpleasant as the alarm is, it does its job of saving lives. The Holy Spirit has many jobs, including one that isn't all that popular—conviction. Conviction is the feeling that follows sin. We have done something wrong and we know it. Remorse, guilt, regret, and the rest of the emotional stew that follows sin is well known. Despite our outward actions, inwardly we're troubled, consumed by shame. All of that is good news.

How can such unsettling feelings be good? First, it reminds us of the presence of the Holy Spirit in our lives. The Holy Spirit is our fire alarm, and as long as we remain open to His work we can avoid repeating past mistakes. That uncomfortable sensation is conviction, and conviction can be our friend. It alerts us to our failings and motivates us to seek reconciliation. Recognition of any problem is the first step to a solution.

Conviction also proves a point: We are part of the family of God. If it were not so, misbehavior would not bother us, and we could dismiss it with little thought and no concern. When we feel conviction it is proof of the Holy Spirit's work, a work He does in the hearts and the minds of believers. Of course, we don't sin just to prove our salvation, but since everyone sins, it is good to know that the conviction we feel is God reaching out, saying, "You still belong." The Holy Spirit does His work for our good. The author of the New Testament letter to the Hebrews summed it up: "Our fathers disciplined us for a little while as they thought best; but God disciplines us for our good, that we may share in his holiness" (12:10 NIV).

Conviction is a course correction to keep us from straying; it is the fire alarm that reminds us that God cares. Have you sinned? You're not alone. Address it; understand that persistent feeling of guilt is your fire alarm. Now that you're aware of the problem and who it is that alerts you to it, then you can take the problem to God in prayer, receive forgiveness, and feel good that God loved you enough to be involved in your life.

The Holy Spirit
Personal Fire Alarm

What Matters Most...

- ◎ Understanding that conviction is a good thing. The feeling may be uncomfortable, but the convicting work of the Holy Spirit is a sign of love.

- ◎ Knowing that everyone sins. Only Christ was sinless on this earth. Everyone else struggles with sin. You are not alone in your sin.

- ◎ Tuning into the Spirit's work in your life. Choosing to open the doors of your mind and heart to His leadership is choosing to open your future to happiness, purpose, and meaning.

- ◎ Discovering that God cares enough to correct. Children are corrected when the need arises, and God corrects you in the same way. Both are done out of love.

What **Doesn't** Matter...

- ◎ Past sins. Everyone has them. Seek forgiveness and let the past go. Several times Jesus said, "Your sins are forgiven. Go and sin no more." It was great advice then, and it still is now.

- ◎ Embarrassment. Embarrassment is good if it brings about a positive change. Beyond that it is useless.

- ◎ The view that if it feels good, do it. God has higher principles, and the Holy Spirit guides you into them. The godly view is to do what is right no matter how it feels.

Focus Points...

The kingdom of God is not a matter of eating and drinking, but of righteousness, peace and joy in the Holy Spirit.
ROMANS 14:17 NIV

The church throughout all Judea and Galilee and Samaria enjoyed peace, being built up; and going on in the fear of the Lord and in the comfort of the Holy Spirit, it continued to increase.
ACTS 9:31 NASB

If your sinful nature controls your mind, there is death. But if the Holy Spirit controls your mind, there is life and peace.
ROMANS 8:6 NLT

May the God of hope fill you with all joy and peace in believing, that you may abound in hope by the power of the Holy Spirit.
ROMANS 15:13 NKJV

what really counts

We through the Spirit wait for the hope of righteousness by faith.
GALATIANS 5:5 KJV

The Holy Spirit convicts of sin, man does not.
OSWALD CHAMBERS

Those who have never felt anxiety on account of their sins are in the most dangerous condition of all.
JOHN TAULER

73

What Matters Most to Me About
The Holy Spirit

The Holy Spirit is not confined to the spiritual shadows of our lives—He is active, involved, and personal to the believer. He was involved in every area of Jesus' ministry and can be involved in every area of your life.

◎ *The Holy Spirit has many descriptive names: Helper, Comforter, Pledge, Seal, and many more. Each name tells something about His work. How does it change your life knowing that the Holy Spirit is there to guide you?*

_____

_____

_____

_____

_____

_____

_____

◎ *The person who places his or her faith in Christ is never alone. Loneliness is a familiar feeling to most people. Knowing the Holy Spirit is close changes your outlook. How does knowing that you're never alone change your view of life?*

_____

_____

_____

_____

_____

_____

_____

what
really
counts

When a person sins, he feels guilt and shame, which is proof that God cares enough to be involved. Repentance rids you of guilty feelings, and that is the goal of the Holy Spirit. What would you like changed from shame to forgiveness?

_____

_____

_____

_____

_____

_____

_____

_____

The Holy Spirit guides you if you allow Him to do so. What decisions are you facing that could benefit from the guiding wisdom of the Holy Spirit?

_____

_____

_____

_____

_____

_____

_____

_____

Every time we say, "I believe in the Holy Spirit," we mean that we believe that there is a living God able and willing to enter human personality and change it.

J. B. PHILLIPS

FAITH

An Introduction

> I have been crucified with Christ; and it is no longer I who live, but Christ lives in me; and the life which I now live in the flesh I live by faith in the Son of God, who loved me and gave Himself up for me.
>
> GALATIANS 2:20 NASB

what really counts

What is the most beautiful thing you've ever seen? Was it a wild, panoramic scene from nature? Maybe it was an unforgettable painting. Or maybe it was a sculpture with exquisite detail. Perhaps it was your child being born. Could you describe what you saw? Can you put into words what you experienced, the emotions you felt, the intellectual challenge that rose up in you? Probably not.

Words fail us when we encounter the remarkable. Even the best authors can create sentences and build paragraphs that paint unforgettable pictures on your mind, but they are always incomplete. The way it works in books is that the writer does his best to make things clear, but the reader must contribute to the process. Faith is like that too.

That's the challenge of faith: it is easier to experience than to explain. You encounter faith. You incorporate faith into your life, and you are forever changed. You bring something to the process, just as a reader does with a novel. The writer can do only so much. The rest is up to the reader.

Faith is an adventure with a discernible beginning and a joyous end. Faith is the most revolutionary idea the world has ever known, and it has been changing lives since the beginning of time. No force in the world is greater and no tool more important than personal, practiced faith. It has been changing lives for centuries; it is changing lives today.

> Faith is deliberate confidence in the character of God whose ways you may not understand at the time.
>
> OSWALD CHAMBERS

Faith
Uncovering the Power

> Faith is the assurance of things hoped for, the conviction of things not seen.
>
> HEBREWS 11:1 NASB

what really counts

Visitors to White Sands, New Mexico, encounter an unusual sight: Poking out of the blistering sand are what look like stunted trees measuring only four to ten feet tall. Many visitors don't realize that the trees are fully grown cottonwoods. If they could push aside the sand, they could see the full height of the trees. The shifting mounds of sand hide much of the tree from view. If a tree atop a thirty-foot sand dune appears ten feet tall, it is in reality forty feet high. The trees can grow as long as a portion of their limbs and leaves reaches the sunlight.

Faith is like that. Faith might seem to some as a belief to add to life, whereas to others who have experienced it, it is life itself. So important is the concept of faith that the word *faith* appears nearly 250 times in the New Testament. Despite these many mentions, its meaning is often misunderstood. Faith is not mere feeling, and it is more than just belief. Some think faith means trusting in something you can't see. It's so much more than that. Faith is "assurance" and "conviction." *Assurance* is another word for "confidence," and *conviction* means "commitment to truth." In other words, faith is as much intellectual as it is emotional. To define it with a handful of words: *faith* means "to be convinced of truth and to live in that certainty."

That's where the rubber of our lives meets the road. We are what we believe. Faith in God means to know He's there and to live accordingly. Faith refuses to treat the spiritual life as if it were a mere ornament of our existence. Faith realizes that God is, that God loves, that God is involved, and that we should connect to God in a personal way—no abstract theology; no confusing religious babble, just you and God making a personal connection. That's what matters. To believe in God is a great start; to have a relationship with Him is the way to live. Faith says, "I will do more than believe; I will live in a way that shows I believe." We may not have all the answers, but we have enough to act on what we know. That act is faith. Like the cottonwoods at White Sands, we are more than we appear. No matter how much sand the world shifts our way, we can be rooted in faith. Faith is a choice. It begins with a conversation between you and God.

Faith
Uncovering the Power

What Matters Most...

◎ Knowing that faith needs both your brain and your heart.

◎ Choosing to discover and value faith.

◎ Knowing there are plenty of reasons to believe and then acting on that knowledge.

◎ Seeing faith as a gift from God and refusing to waste it.

◎ Knowing that faith empowers, enables, and comes from a personal encounter with God.

What Doesn't Matter...

◎ Age. Now is the best time to exercise faith—age means nothing.

◎ The past. No one gets to unwind the clock, but everyone can embrace a better future.

◎ Education. College degrees are not required to benefit from faith; applied belief is all that you need.

◎ Someone's approval. Faith is always about the individual encountering God. You are that individual.

◎ History. Background, bad decisions, financial reversals, regrets are anchors; faith is the wind in our sails. It frees us from the past.

Focus Points...

Behold, as for the proud one, his soul is not right within him; but the righteous will live by his faith.
HABAKKUK 2:4 NASB

Some men brought to him a paralytic, lying on a mat. When Jesus saw their faith, he said to the paralytic, "Take heart, son; your sins are forgiven."
MATTHEW 9:2 NIV

Jesus answered and said to them, "Have faith in God."
MARK 11:22 NKJV

I did this so that you might trust the power of God rather than human wisdom.
1 CORINTHIANS 2:5 NLT

what really counts

You, dear friends, must continue to build your lives on the foundation of your holy faith. And continue to pray as you are directed by the Holy Spirit.
JUDE 20 NLT

A little faith will bring your soul to heaven, but a lot of faith will bring heaven to your soul.

DWIGHT L. MOODY

Faith is not a refuge from reality. It is a demand that we face reality, with all its difficulties, opportunities, and implications.

EVELYN UNDERHILL

Faith
Unleashing the Power

Without faith it is impossible to please Him, for he who comes to God must believe that He is and that He is a rewarder of those who seek Him.

HEBREWS 11:6 NASB

The famous British soldier Oliver Cromwell quipped, "Put your trust in God—but keep your powder dry." Today the statement strikes us as funny, but there is some truth to it. Soldiers on the front line of battle needed faith, but they also needed to be actively involved in the fight. Their lives and the lives of their companions depended on it. Although closely related, faith is more than belief; it is belief applied to thoughts and actions. It is more than feeling, more than hope, more than adopted principles; it is a choice of belief and behavior. Faith in motion is power unleashed.

The New Testament is a collection of twenty-seven books written by God-inspired men. One book—Hebrews—holds a special chapter devoted to the principles of faith. The chapter surprises some who expect such a topic to be nothing more than dusty theology. Instead, they find a list of people from every walk of life—from farmers to fugitives to a former harlot—all whose lives were changed by faith. Students of the Bible often refer to this chapter as the Hall of Faith. There is a rock-and-roll hall of fame in Cleveland, Ohio; a football hall of fame in Canton, Ohio; and a baseball version in Cooperstown, New York. Every year, thousands of visitors make their way through the exhibit-crowded halls to learn more about their favorite sports and rock stars. When it comes to understanding the history of faith, people turn to the eleventh chapter of Hebrews.

Reading the passage a few times causes a pattern to stand out. The pattern can be expressed in two words: *by faith*. Name follows name; event follows event; and all of them are related to an action: Abel *offered*; Enoch *obtained*; Noah *prepared*; Abraham *obeyed*; and so on. For these heroes, faith was something to unleash, a power to release. Their heroics were rooted in action and fueled by belief. That's where their heroism lay—in unleashing their faith so it became active belief.

A bridge is useless until someone crosses it; a chair may be lovely in design, but it doesn't live up to its potential until someone rests his weight in it. You become what God has always meant you to be when you let faith guide, motivate, and empower your daily actions. Faith is not faith if left on the shelf. It should be present at work; should permeate the home; and be utilized in every major decision. Believe, and then act on that belief.

Faith
Unleashing the Power

What Matters Most...

- ◎ Understanding that *faith* is more than a noun; it is a life-changing verb. Action is one of the main ingredients in faith.

- ◎ Knowing that belief in your mind becomes faith in your heart; faith in your heart becomes faith in your day-to-day life.

- ◎ Every morning is a new opportunity to exercise faith.

- ◎ Active faith changes a person; active faith also changes the world.

- ◎ The choice is yours to unleash the power of energetic faith. It is a choice only you can make.

What Doesn't Matter...

- ◎ Fear. The antidote to fear is faith. Fear is an emotion; faith is a fact.

- ◎ Detractors. There are always those who find fault and offer criticism. Faith doesn't listen to them.

- ◎ Setbacks. Faith does not mean a perfect life. Faith is empowerment in difficulty. It is what gets you through.

- ◎ Questions. No one understands it all, but you can understand enough to believe and let that belief become vibrant, life-changing faith.

- ◎ Yesterday. You can utilize faith today, changing your view of your past and your hope for the future.

Focus Points...

I have fought the good fight, I have finished the course, I have kept the faith; in the future there is laid up for me the crown of righteousness, which the Lord, the righteous Judge, will award to me on that day; and not only to me, but also to all who have loved His appearing.

2 Timothy 4:7–8 NASB

We always thank God, the Father of our Lord Jesus Christ, when we pray for you, because we have heard of your faith in Christ Jesus and of the love you have for all the saints— the faith and love that spring from the hope that is stored up for you in heaven and that you have already heard about in the word of truth, the gospel that has come to you.

Colossians 1:3–6 NIV

When Jesus saw their faith, He said to the paralytic, "Son, your sins are forgiven you."

Mark 2:5 NKJV

what really counts

Whatsoever is born of God overcometh the world: and this is the victory that overcometh the world, even our faith.

1 John 5:4 KJV

Faith means believing in realities that go beyond sense and sight . . . being aware of unseen divine realities all around you.

Joni Eareckson Tada

Faith is not a feeling; it is action. It is a willed choice.

Elisabeth Elliot

85

What Matters Most to Me About
Faith

Faith is like a muscle; it needs exercise. Below are a few suggestions to follow to make daily faith more real:

◉ *"I will look upward."* Faith must be aimed, and since God is the originator of faith, He is the object of faith. Start with Him; continue with Him; end with Him. Make a commitment today to include God in your decision making, choosing several areas to exercise your faith.

_____

_____

_____

_____

_____

_____

_____

_____

◉ *"I will look inward."* Faith resides in your heart and mind. Give it thought so that it roots in the brain; commit to it so that it grows in your heart. What is keeping you from embracing faith today?

_____

_____

_____

_____

_____

_____

_____

what
really
counts

◎ *"I will look outward."* Faith not only changes you, but it also affects those around you: family, friends, fellow employees, clients—everyone you meet. List three areas where you can apply faith to your public life.

_____

_____

_____

_____

_____

_____

_____

◎ *"I will look onward."* Faith changes you one day at a time. The future is always brighter with faith. What commitment can you make today to move you forward on the path of faith?

_____

_____

_____

_____

_____

_____

_____

_____

FAITH

Faith comes from hearing, and hearing by the word of Christ.
ROMANS 10:17 NASB

LOVE

An Introduction

> Dear friends, let us love one another, for love comes from God. Everyone who loves has been born of God and knows God.
>
> 1 JOHN 4:7 NIV

what really counts

The apostle Paul was not always a Christian. In fact, he was one of the early persecutors of the church. By his own admission, he was "once a blasphemer and a persecutor and a violent man" (1 Timothy 1:13 NIV). Later in life he would write what may well be one of the most beautiful passages ever penned. First Corinthians 13 is often called the Love Chapter. How does a man whose driving compulsion is to eradicate every Christian from the face of the earth become one of the faith's greatest spokesmen and authors? The love of Christ is what made the difference.

During the 1960s, Kim Casali began drawing pictures of a little girl and boy and captioning them with charming phrases that always began "Love is ..." In the

1970s those drawings began to appear on the comic pages of the world's newspapers. Today they remain the favorite of millions. Love is more than most of us imagine it to be. It goes far beyond comic-page proverbs. It is defined and illustrated in the pages of the Bible, and that kind of love is life-changing.

One of the things that really counts in life is outward-bound love, love that goes beyond songs, poems, and feelings, love that is stimulated by a desire to see someone else happy. Love is more than most people understand. Let's learn what the apostle Paul meant when he said, "Love never fails."

Love is the beauty of the soul.

SAINT AUGUSTINE

Love
Love Is

Let all that you do be done with love.
1 Corinthians 16:14 NKJV

what really counts

Love is . . . everywhere. It is the topic of songs in every type of music. One of the best-selling genres in literature is romance. Children speak words of love to parents, and parents speak words of love to children. The word *love* describes the emotion shared by family and couples and is even a euphemism for *sex*. It is one of the most frequently used words. Sometimes it is an honest expression of a true feeling; other times it is little more than an emotional club. And here is the irony. This ubiquitous word is so seldom understood and is almost impossible to define, and yet we all know it when we see it and feel it.

Love is . . . more than a feeling. Take a poll and ask, "What is love?" and you're likely to hear descriptions but no definitions. Love is described as a feeling in the stomach or the heart. It's true; we *feel* love. It is, after all, an emotion. Emotion is the compound of *e*, meaning "inside," and *motion*, indicating "movement." When we feel an emotion, we are moved on the inside. There is a physical sensation. But love goes beyond that.

Love is . . . the essence of God. Love is desiring the best for the ones loved. It is a hunger to see them well and happy. Love is the indefinable expression of goodwill. The apostle John was a disciple of Christ. He served the faith and often suffered for it. He is known as the apostle of love because love permeated everything he taught. When he was an enfeebled, elderly man too weak to walk to church, he requested to be carried there, and every Sunday he had a single message for the congregation: "Little children, love one another." It was and is the life motto for people of faith. John also said something that forces us to rethink our definition of love. He wrote, "God is love." God does more than love; He *is* love. To sense love, to express love, is to encounter God.

Love is more than we think. It's the power that changes us and changes others. It is a conduit of God's care. Ancient Rome built an extensive network of aqueducts that brought thirty-eight million gallons of water into the city every day. Strength, confidence, and comfort come to us through the conduit of God's love. The choice is ours to open the floodgates and to know that God's desire is to love us.

Love
Love Is

What Matters Most...

◎ Knowing that God is the Author of love. As the Author, He is the One who knows most about it. In fact, it defines Him. To know love is to know the Author of love.

◎ Knowing that love is more than what you feel—it is the way you think. Of all the things that motivate you, love is one that changes you from within.

◎ Knowing that love is a choice, not an emotion. Choosing to love requires commitment and a conscious decision.

◎ The key to loving others is to first love yourself. This is not selfish love that comes at the expense of others; it is the simple understanding that self-hatred can never give rise to love.

What **Doesn't** Matter...

◎ The world's view of love. Television, movies, and popular songs are entertaining, but they seldom teach the truth about love. God's definition and example of love is the one to follow.

◎ Return on investment. Businesses are concerned with return on investment, but love acts without expectation. Love is expressed because it is the right thing to do and not because it will bring some kind of payment.

◎ Feeling. Love is an emotion, but it is not only an emotion. Feelings change with circumstances, but love never changes. It is never altered by circumstance. Instead, it changes everything around it.

Focus Points...

A new commandment I give to you, that you love one another, even as I have loved you, that you also love one another. By this all men will know that you are My disciples, if you have love for one another.
JOHN 13:34–35 NASB

Let no debt remain outstanding, except the continuing debt to love one another, for he who loves his fellowman has fulfilled the law.
ROMANS 13:8 NIV

Though I bestow all my goods to feed the poor, and though I give my body to be burned, but have not love, it profits me nothing.
1 CORINTHIANS 13:3 NKJV

what really counts

There are three things that will endure—faith, hope, and love—and the greatest of these is love.
1 CORINTHIANS 13:13 NLT

As touching brotherly love ye need not that I write unto you: for ye yourselves are taught of God to love one another.
1 THESSALONIANS 4:9 KJV

To love is to will the good of another.
SAINT THOMAS AQUINAS

We can do no great things; only small things with great love.
MOTHER TERESA

93

Love

Love Does

> Be imitators of God, therefore, as dearly loved children and live a life of love, just as Christ loved us and gave himself up for us as a fragrant offering and sacrifice to God.
>
> EPHESIANS 5:1–2 NIV

what really counts

Like all of us, the great man of God Saint Francis of Assisi had fears. He feared leprosy, that contagious disease that costs the victim everything. In Francis's day, it was a condemnation of death. One day, he was walking down a narrow path when he looked up to see the frightening white skin of a leper. He recoiled, but shame overcame him. Francis of Assisi reined in his fear and then did what few men could. He approached the afflicted man, threw his arms around him, and gave him the customary kiss. He then moved down the path only to turn a moment later to see the leper one more time. The man was gone. For the rest of his life, Francis maintained that it was Christ he met on the road that day.

What can fill a man with that kind of courage? Love can. Not emotional love, but the kind of love that shows itself in action. *Love* is more verb than noun, more action than feeling, and more outward than inward. The ancient Greeks used three words for love: *eros* for erotic emotions; *philos* for friendship; and *agape*. The New Testament uses this last word to describe the kind of love that God has for us and that we should have for one another. It is unselfish love and always has the good of someone else in mind.

In 1875 the painter Marcel de Leclure wrote a love letter. He used the French phrase *je vous aime* 1,875,000 times—1,000 times the years of the 1875 calendar. He recited the phrase while a hired scribe wrote it over and over again. It may be the world's longest love letter. God wrote a love letter called the Bible. From its first words to its last, it is a reminder of His great love. Not just the feeling, but the action. God acted on His love. Jesus died for us because of His love. Love does. In word, love does; in action, love does; in thinking, love does.

Jesus said, "I am giving you a new commandment: Love each other. Just as I have loved you, you should love each other" (John 13:34 NLT). This could be considered the eleventh commandment. Jesus didn't give it as a suggestion or a hint; He gave it as a command. We are to love one another in the same manner Jesus loved us; and He loved us in action, not just in word.

Love
Love Does

What Matters Most...

◎ Facing the things you fear in love. Love is empowering. It steels the spine and settles the heart, enabling you to do the difficult.

◎ Knowing that anything done for someone in love is something also done for God. Love is God's tool, one He's given you to use in life.

◎ Love is an action. It doesn't wait for a feeling; it does what needs to be done. Love is defined by what it does, not by what it feels like.

◎ Love is a commandment, not a suggestion. Jesus gave what many now call the eleventh commandment—that you should love one another as He loved you. He set the example.

What **Doesn't** Matter...

◎ Emotions. Emotions are important, but they work without direction or purpose. Choosing love requires the mind as well as the heart.

◎ Fears. Love conquers fear and casts out anxiety. Life will continue to throw concerns your way, but godly love will be your defense.

◎ Past failures. It's never too late to start loving. A lifetime of bitterness may have preceded this moment, but the rest of life and all of eternity remains to pour out love.

Focus Points...

Let us hold unswervingly to the hope we profess, for he who promised is faithful. And let us consider how we may spur one another on toward love and good deeds.
HEBREWS 10:23–24 NIV

You were called to freedom, brethren; only do not turn your freedom into an opportunity for the flesh, but through love serve one another.
GALATIANS 5:13 NASB

May the Lord make your love grow and overflow to each other and to everyone else, just as our love overflows toward you.
1 THESSALONIANS 3:12 NLT

what really counts

Continue to love each other with true Christian love. Don't forget to show hospitality to strangers, for some who have done this have entertained angels without realizing it!
HEBREWS 13:1–2 NLT

My little children, let us not love in word, neither in tongue; but in deed and in truth.
1 JOHN 3:18 KJV

There is no love which does not become help.
PAUL TILLICH

God regards with how much love a person performs a work, rather than how much he does.
THOMAS À KEMPIS

97

What Matters Most to Me About
Love

Henry Drummond said, "Love is not a thing of enthusiastic emotion. It is a rich, strong, manly, vigorous expression of the whole round Christian character—the Christlike nature in its fullest development. And the constituents of this great character are only to be built up by ceaseless practice." Love takes practice. Take a few moments to personalize godly love.

◎ *Love takes work, and it takes practice. The trick is finding your personal problem areas. In what areas are you least likely to love? Jot down a few.*

_____

_____

_____

_____

_____

_____

_____

◎ *Love has always been a choice. Think of a few recent times in which a love response would have been better than what was done and write them down.*

_____

_____

_____

_____

_____

_____

⊙ *If love had been your constant choice, how would your life be different today? Would you be different? Would friends and family be different? List a few ways your life would be different than it is now.*

_____

_____

_____

_____

_____

_____

_____

_____

⊙ *Jesus said that you must love your neighbors as yourself. That means you must first love yourself before you can share love with anyone else. What keeps you from experiencing that healthy self-appreciation that God intends? List several things and then cross them out, replacing them with the positive counterpart.*

_____

_____

_____

_____

_____

_____

_____

_____

He does much who loves much.
THOMAS À KEMPIS

HEAVEN

An Introduction

> Blessed be the God and Father of our Lord Jesus Christ! According to his great mercy, he has caused us to be born again to a living hope through the resurrection of Jesus Christ from the dead, to an inheritance that is imperishable, undefiled, and unfading, kept in heaven for you.
>
> 1 PETER 1:3–4 ESV

what really counts

A little girl was looking at the stars one night with her mother. The beauty of the night touched her, and she asked, "If heaven is this beautiful on the wrong side, what must it be like on the other side?" Humans have powerful imaginations. Novels are written, movies made, poetry penned, paintings brushed on canvas, and sculptures crafted, yet no matter how creative and imaginative we are, we still have trouble picturing heaven.

Heaven is a promised place with doors open for the person of faith. It is the reward promised to us by God. What we do here on earth affects what we experience in heaven. Our works here build up rewards there. The Bible describes it in general but not in detail. It is beyond our understanding, but it is real nonetheless. There we experience God and life with eyes that see better and minds that understand more. No pain there, no sorrow, and no illness. It is life as originally designed.

Imagine a sinless world. Imagine an uncorrupted world. Imagine a world where time doesn't age us, where disease can't touch us, and where sin is a thing of the past. Imagine a place perfectly suited to you and you to it.

No matter how many questions we have; no matter how much knowledge we feel we lack, there is an inner witness that there is more beyond our senses, a place we long to be. Heaven isn't a myth; it is the destiny and reward for believers.

> Hearts on earth say in the course of a joyful experience, "I don't want this ever to end." But it invariably does. The hearts of those in heaven say, "I want this to go on forever." And it will. There is no better news than this.
>
> J. I. PACKER

Heaven
The Way It Was Meant to Be

> [Jesus said,] "Pray, then, in this way: 'Our Father who is in heaven, hallowed be Your name. Your kingdom come. Your will be done, on earth as it is in heaven.'"
>
> MATTHEW 6:9–10 NASB

what really counts

When Jesus stood before the massive crowd that had gathered to hear Him deliver what we now call the Sermon on the Mount, He taught us how to pray. He did so by modeling a prayer. Today, we call that model the Lord's Prayer. Many people can recite it from memory, and almost everyone has heard it. Tucked away in its few sentences is the phrase "Your will be done, on earth as it is in heaven." It's an odd phrase. Jesus taught that we should include in our prayers a request that God's will in heaven be God's will on earth.

But what goes on in heaven? What is heaven? Where is heaven? Why should we care? For every answer there are ten more questions. That's because heaven defies description. The best philosophers, poets, and writers could never do it justice. Nonetheless, it is real. It is the place where God dwells and where Christians arrive after death. It is a place of purpose, of fulfillment, of challenge, and of unfettered worship. It is a place free of the restrictions this life presents.

All of those things are good, but there's a danger in seeing heaven as a mere amusement park. It is a destination to a place and to a person. Heaven is the way life was meant to be. It remains the ideal that once existed in the Garden of Eden.

The Statue of Liberty is one the world's best-known figures. Given to the United States by the French, the grand lady stands with torch held high. At the base are the words written by Emma Lazarus: "Give me your tired, your poor, your huddled masses yearning to breathe free, the wretched refuse of your teeming shore, send these, the homeless, tempest-tossed, to me: I lift my lamp beside the golden door." Those same words could be written on the doorposts of heaven. It is God's place for the world's huddled masses, and Christ made it possible for us to live there. But heaven isn't a someday thing, it resides in every person of faith. Christ has opened the doors for us to begin to experience some of heaven on earth and has prepared us to see it one day in all its grandeur. The best way to begin the experience is to pray as Jesus taught us, that God's will be done on earth as it is in heaven.

Heaven
The Way It Was Meant to Be

What Matters Most...

◉ Knowing that there is more beyond this life and that Christ made it possible.

◉ Believing that Christ is the key that unlocks heaven's doors.

◉ Understanding that heaven is beyond description but not beyond experience.

◉ Choosing to see God's will done on earth as it is in heaven.

◉ Living today as if eternity is just around the corner.

What Doesn't Matter...

◉ Unanswered questions. Not only do you not know it all, you can't—yet.

◉ Death. You don't seek out death, but it need not be frightening. Death is promotion day.

◉ Wealth or poverty. Heaven isn't based on what you have but on whom you know.

◉ Time. Here, time is limited; there, time isn't. Heaven is eternal, just as you will be.

◉ Good works. Good works are important, but it is the work of Christ that makes the difference.

Focus Points...

Store up for yourselves treasures in heaven, where neither moth nor rust destroys, and where thieves do not break in or steal; for where your treasure is, there your heart will be also.
MATTHEW 6:20–21 NASB

We know that if the earthly tent we live in is destroyed, we have a building from God, an eternal house in heaven, not built by human hands.
2 CORINTHIANS 5:1 NIV

Let heaven fill your thoughts. Do not think only about things down here on earth. For you died when Christ died, and your real life is hidden with Christ in God.
COLOSSIANS 3:2–3 NLT

what really counts

Henceforth there is laid up for me a crown of righteousness, which the Lord, the righteous judge, shall give me at that day: and not to me only, but unto all them also that love his appearing.
2 TIMOTHY 4:8 KJV

My knowledge of that life is small, the eye of faith is dim; but 'tis enough that Christ knows all, and I shall be with him.

RICHARD BAXTER

Heaven will be the perfection we have always longed for. All the things that made Earth unlovely and tragic will be absent in Heaven.

BILLY GRAHAM

Heaven
More Than Pie in the Sky

He has made everything beautiful in its time. He has also set eternity in the hearts of men; yet they cannot fathom what God has done from beginning to end.

ECCLESIASTES 3:11 NIV

what really counts

"Every human heart yearns for not only a person but a place. The place we were made for." Randy Alcorn wrote those words. He is a man who thinks constantly of heaven and, by doing so, has helped many people understand their earthly lives better. He said, "A robust, accurate, and biblically energized view of heaven will bring you a new spiritual passion."

God has put a hunger for heaven in our hearts, not to pacify us but to encourage us. Heaven is not a carrot on a stick dangled before us so that we will be good. We strive to be good because it is right and it pleases God. Heaven is a reward for faith, not for works, not for achievement, but for true belief. There is a twist about heaven that many people miss. While it is true that heaven is a reward for those who trust God, it is also a reward for God Himself. To have us with Him brings Him joy. Our heaven is His heaven too. As Jesus said, "If anyone loves Me, he will keep My word; and My

HEAVEN

Father will love him, and We will come to him and make Our abode with him" (John 14:23 NASB). Heaven is in our hearts, and our hearts and souls are in heaven.

A. W. Tozer called heaven "the long tomorrow" and said we do well to think on it. Of course, we have questions about the details; heaven doesn't come with a color brochure. The one thing that makes it all worthwhile is that Jesus is there. Jesus comforted His disciples with the promise of what was to come. It's the same promise given to people of faith. "In My Father's house are many mansions; if it were not so, I would have told you. I go to prepare a place for you. And if I go and prepare a place for you, I will come again and receive you to Myself; that where I am, there you may be also" (John 14:2–3 NKJV).

Max Lucado said, "Believe me when I say it will be worth it. No cost is too high. If you must pay a price, pay it! No sacrifice is too much. If you must leave baggage on the trail, leave it! No loss will compare. Whatever it takes, do it. For heaven's sake." Let's live every day for heaven's sake.

Heaven
More Than Pie in the Sky

What Matters Most...

◎ Recognizing the inward hunger for God and His heaven.

◎ Thinking beyond this moment, the day, this month and year, and beginning to think about the "long tomorrow."

◎ Knowing that faith makes you a citizen in two worlds, one that lasts an eternity.

◎ The price for heaven was impossibly expensive, but Jesus paid it for you on the cross.

◎ Realizing that the choice of faith not only changes your today, but also your eternal tomorrows.

What Doesn't Matter...

◎ The length of this life. You do not have the promise of tomorrow in this world, but you do have the promise of eternity.

◎ Sight. Seeing is not always believing. Spiritual sight helps you catch a glimpse of the glory to come.

◎ Things in this life left undone. No one does life perfectly. There will always be things you wished you had done.

◎ Things earned and lost here. Joy and sorrow walk with everyone. In heaven your treasures cannot be destroyed or lost.

◎ Fear of punishment. God's desire is to replace fear with joy. Heaven is His way of reuniting the family.

Focus Points…

He was saying, "Jesus, remember me when You come in Your kingdom!" And He said to him, "Truly I say to you, today you shall be with Me in Paradise."
LUKE 23:42–43 NASB

He who has an ear, let him hear what the Spirit says to the churches. To him who overcomes, I will give the right to eat from the tree of life, which is in the paradise of God.
REVELATION 2:7 NIV

We are always confident, knowing that while we are at home in the body we are absent from the Lord. For we walk by faith, not by sight. We are confident, yes, well pleased rather to be absent from the body and to be present with the Lord.
2 CORINTHIANS 5:6–8 NKJV

what really counts

God blesses those who work for peace, for they will be called the children of God. God blesses those who are persecuted because they live for God, for the Kingdom of Heaven is theirs.
MATTHEW 5:9–10 NLT

Has this world been so kind to you that you should leave with regret? There are better things ahead than any we leave behind.

C. S. LEWIS

The main object of religion is not to get a man into heaven, but to get heaven into him.

THOMAS HARDY

109

What Matters Most to Me About
Heaven

Looking forward to heaven isn't escapism; it is a way to get your spiritual bearings. Heaven isn't a goal; it's a promised reward for faith placed in Christ.

◉ *Broaden your thinking to include heaven. It is easy to get lost in the pressures of today and have no room to think about tomorrow, but tomorrow arrives and so will the endless tomorrows we call heaven. Write down a few ways in which the knowledge of heaven changes your view of your world.*

_____

_____

_____

_____

_____

_____

_____

◉ *To be in heaven is to be in the undiminished presence of God. In some ways, life on earth is practice for heaven. Jot down a few ways you might live for God this week as though you were in heaven now.*

_____

_____

_____

_____

_____

_____

what
really
counts

◎ *Some think of heaven as being far away, but it is just a breath away. In fact, you can see bits of heaven in your daily life. How has God blessed you? List a few things that you feel God has done for you.*

_____

_____

_____

_____

_____

_____

_____

_____

◎ *Heaven is usually seen as a reward you will receive. While that is true, your presence in heaven will please God. While it is your desire to spend eternity with Him, it is His desire to spend eternity with you. How does that knowledge make you feel?*

_____

_____

_____

_____

_____

_____

_____

You do this because you are looking forward to the joys of heaven—as you have been ever since you first heard the truth of the Good News.

COLOSSIANS 1:5 NLT

GOD'S WORD

An Introduction

> Remember Jesus Christ, raised from the dead, descended from David. This is my gospel, for which I am suffering even to the point of being chained like a criminal. But God's word is not chained.
>
> 2 TIMOTHY 2:8–9 NIV

what really counts

No book has been so revered as the Bible, yet no book has endured so much attack as the Bible. This collection of writings is inspired by God through men to us. It is useful in every area of life. Many people have attacked it, saying that it is out of date, inaccurate, and meaningless. Yet the Bible has proved its detractors wrong and itself right. The great patriot Patrick Henry said, "The Bible is worth all other books which have ever been printed." The Bible is owned by millions and read by millions. It has been translated into almost every existing language.

What makes the book unique is its origin in God and His protection of it through the centuries. The last book of the New Testament was written almost twenty centuries ago. That may seem so long ago in the past that the writing could have no bearing on the twenty-first-century world, but it does. Every day, millions of people pick up a Bible and read. It isn't always an easy book, but it is always a life-changing book.

To open the Bible is to peek into the mind of God, to hear His heart, and to know His thoughts. Studying the Bible is as much an honor as an obligation. The Bible is no ordinary book; it is God's wisdom for today, bound in a cover. It has been changing lives for millennia and will continue to do so until Jesus comes again.

> The Bible is not only a book which I can understand, it is a book which understands me.
>
> EMILE CAILLIET

God's Word
Finding Truth, Avoiding Error

The word of God is living and active and sharper than any two-edged sword, and piercing as far as the division of soul and spirit, of both joints and marrow, and able to judge the thoughts and intentions of the heart.

HEBREWS 4:12 NASB

what really counts

We are familiar with maps. We use them to plan trips, learn more of the world, describe geography, and more. The earliest maps come from the Babylonians twenty-three hundred years before Christ. Without an accurate map, it is easy to get lost on a long trip. Life is much harder to plan. With its ups and downs and unexpected terrain, life can have some confusing turns. We could use a good map. In a sense, that is what the Bible is—a map from the past that shows the right path for today and tomorrow.

The word *Bible* simply means "book." It comes from the name of the ancient city of Byblos where paper was made from reeds. When the word *Bible* is used, it refers to the writing material, the pages. *Scripture* is another word often used to refer to the Bible. *Scripture* ("script") refers to the actual writing, to the meaning. The Bible is often called the *Word of God*. That's a fitting description, for it contains the spoken and inspired words of God in its pages.

We live in a marvelous time. Where once a Bible would cost a year's wages, we can now purchase copies for a few dollars or even read it on the Internet. There are many translations to choose from. There are Bibles geared for serious students, beginners, and children. Added to that are audio Bibles that allow us to have the Scriptures read to us. Even so, the best-selling book in the world is often forgotten or ignored. Too often there is more dust than fingerprints on our Bibles.

Abraham Lincoln wasn't a theologian or a preacher, but he was a man who came to respect the guiding, encouraging, correcting, life-changing truth found in the Bible. "I believe," he said, "the Bible is the best gift God has ever given to man. All the good from the Savior of the world is communicated to us through this book." What he knew is what we need to know: God has given us a book like no other, one that changes minds, opens hearts, heals hurts, lights darkness, straightens paths, and shows us the path to God through Jesus Christ. Paperboys used to stand on street corners with the latest newspaper in their hands, shouting, "Read all about it!" If you want to know God, if you want to have purpose, then read all about it.

God's Word
Finding Truth, Avoiding Error

What Matters Most...

◎ Knowing that the Bible exists for a reason. It has endured because it is more than just a book.

◎ Understanding that the Bible changes lives one at a time.

◎ Seeing God in its pages. You see God clearest through the pages of the Bible.

◎ Realizing that the Bible contains more than historical stories and spiritual advice.

◎ Picking up the Bible and investing time personalizing the truth on its pages.

What **Doesn't** Matter...

◎ A theological education. There are many wonderful teachers and books to help you understand God's Word.

◎ Conviction. Sometimes the Bible shows your sin and your failings. This is good.

◎ Being new to the Bible. Everyone is a novice when it comes to the Bible.

◎ Previously held beliefs. The Bible has changed a lot of minds.

◎ Current trends. The Bible provides a foundation for all your actions and decisions.

Focus Points...

The word of God is living and active and sharper than any two-edged sword, and piercing as far as the division of soul and spirit, of both joints and marrow, and able to judge the thoughts and intentions of the heart.
HEBREWS 4:12 NASB

Jesus replied, "Your problem is that you don't know the Scriptures, and you don't know the power of God."
MATTHEW 22:29 NLT

Beginning at Moses and all the Prophets, He expounded to them in all the Scriptures the things concerning Himself.
LUKE 24:27 NKJV

Knowing this first, that no prophecy of the scripture is of any private interpretation. For the prophecy came not in old time by the will of man: but holy men of God spake as they were moved by the Holy Ghost.
2 PETER 1:20–21 KJV

what really counts

This book outlives, outloves, outlifts, outlasts, outreaches, outruns, and outranks all books. This book is faith producing. It is hope awakening. It is death destroying, and those who embrace it find forgiveness of sin.

A. Z. CONRAD

The Holy Scriptures are our letters from home.

SAINT AUGUSTINE OF HIPPO

God's Word
The Source

> Every word of God is tested; He is a shield to those who take refuge in Him.
>
> PROVERBS 30:5 NASB

The Gulf of Mexico is unique. Near the city of Chicxulub is a multi-ringed impact crater. Scientists from NASA believe an asteroid close to twelve miles across smashed into the earth. The impact was so great that a plume of dust and dirt spread through the atmosphere and brought darkness that lasted six months. That one event changed everything.

The Bible is a book of great impact. Not catastrophic impact such as the Chicxulub event, but an impact that changes everything one person at a time. The Bible is more than a book. It's actually a collection of sixty-six books by more than forty different authors written on three continents over a period of fifteen hundred years. Yet the emphasis isn't on the human authors as with most books, but on the Author who inspired it—God. When it applies to the Bible, the word *inspired* means more than just creative stirring. *Inspired* comes from an ancient Greek word *(theopneustos),* which means "God breathed"; that is, the Bible is a product of God's work. The apostle Paul wrote, "All Scripture is inspired by God and is useful to teach us what is true and to make us realize what is wrong in our lives. It straightens us out and teaches us to do what is right. It is God's way of preparing us in every way, fully equipped for every good thing God wants us to do" (2 Timothy 3:16–17 NLT).

There are many promises in those few lines. There is a promise that what we read in the Bible is not just a human philosophy but the source for our understanding of God. It teaches us what is true, and in a world of confusing opinions, it is wonderful to have a solid source of guidance. The Bible also corrects us. The Scripture is not a list of don'ts as some have portrayed it, but it does contain some prohibitions. A quick study of those doesn't show a killjoy God but a caring One who knows the price of our actions. It also equips us to do good in our world. It shows us what is good and then equips us to do it.

It takes some practice to read the Bible, but the effort is worth it. There is no other book like it. It has been and remains the source for knowledge about God and about ourselves. It is time to feel the impact.

God's Word
The Source

What Matters Most...

◎ Looking for impact. The Bible leaves its mark on those who come to it with a ready and open mind.

◎ Seeing the difference the Bible has made in the lives of others.

◎ Seeing the difference the Bible has made in the world.

◎ Remembering the Bible is inspired—God-breathed. It begins with Him, has Him in the middle, and ends with Him.

◎ The Bible is true, accurate, honest, open, and full of the truth you need.

What **Doesn't** Matter...

◎ Knowing everything in the Bible. Very few people do. Bible study is a process that thankfully never ends.

◎ A single reading. Because God helps you understand His Word, you often find new things in passages you've read before.

◎ Difficulties in life—the Bible has answers and/or words of comfort.

◎ Feeling unique. The Bible holds stories of people who have been through similar or worse situations.

◎ Personal history. Whatever your past, the Bible remains the source of help for the future.

Focus Points...

Your testimonies are wonderful; therefore my soul observes them. The unfolding of Your words gives light; it gives understanding to the simple.
PSALM 119:129–130 NASB

They read from the Book of the Law of God, making it clear and giving the meaning so that the people could understand what was being read.
NEHEMIAH 8:8 NIV

Baruch the son of Neriah did according to all that Jeremiah the prophet commanded him, reading from the book the words of the LORD in the LORD's house.
JEREMIAH 36:8 NKJV

Until I get there, focus on reading the Scriptures to the church, encouraging the believers, and teaching them.
1 TIMOTHY 4:13 NLT

Work hard so God can approve you. Be a good worker, one who does not need to be ashamed and who correctly explains the word of truth.
2 TIMOTHY 2:15 NLT

what really counts

Nobody ever outgrows Scripture; the book widens and deepens with our years.

CHARLES SPURGEON

A man who has deprived himself of the best there is in the world has deprived himself of the Bible.

WOODROW WILSON

121

What Matters Most to Me About
God's Word

Bible study is some of the most rewarding time you can have in your life, and the knowledge you gain lasts an eternity. It will open your eyes, open your heart, and open your mind.

◎ *The best way to judge the power of the Bible is to read it for yourself. If you don't already have a modern translation, go to a Christian bookstore and buy one. If money is a concern, ask for a paperback New Testament. Start with the Gospel of John and read the first four chapters. Each chapter makes a statement about who Jesus is. Write down your impressions.*

_____

_____

_____

_____

_____

_____

_____

_____

◎ *Taking your time, read the entire Gospel of John over the next week or two and make a note of anything that surprises you.*

_____

_____

_____

_____

_____

what
really
counts

⊙ *Attend a Bible-based church this Sunday and listen closely to the sermon. Jot down three or four things you learned from the Bible.*

_____

_____

_____

_____

_____

_____

_____

_____

_____

⊙ *Bible study is especially interesting in a group. Most churches have Sunday morning or midweek Bible studies for all ages. Plan on attending and jot down a few questions to ask.*

_____

_____

_____

_____

_____

_____

_____

_____

_____

Thy word have I hid in mine heart,
that I might not sin against thee.
PSALM 119:11 KJV

THE FUTURE

An Introduction

> Instruct them to do good, to be rich in good works, to be generous and ready to share, storing up for themselves the treasure of a good foundation for the future, so that they may take hold of that which is life indeed.
>
> 1 TIMOTHY 6:18–19 NASB

what really counts

As a child you may have played with one of those wonderful toys made of cardboard and a couple of mirrors, or you may have made one yourself. Two mirrors turned at opposing forty-five-degree angles and enclosed in a square cardboard tube made the perfect periscope. With it we could peek over fences and look around corners. It was great fun. If only we had something that would help us look around the corner of time and see what was coming. The future is on its way. It always has been and always will continue its unending approach. Tomorrow flows into today and will do so until the end of time.

No one can predict the future. Crystal balls are

nothing more than spheres of glass. God, however, knows the beginning from the end. Jesus is described as being the Alpha and the Omega (Revelation 1:8), the first and the last letters of the Greek alphabet. God is the start and the end of everything. He is our past, our present, our future. While it is true that no one can predict the future, God has chosen to reveal some of it to us. Jesus ascended to heaven but promised to return in the same fashion as He left. God, who knows all things, has revealed His will to us to aid us in our daily lives. Because of that, we can see a little ways around the corner—and it doesn't require mirrors.

> Never be afraid to trust an unknown future to a known God.
>
> CORRIE TEN BOOM

The Future
Coming Again

Men of Galilee,...why do you stand here looking into the sky? This same Jesus, who has been taken from you into heaven, will come back in the same way you have seen him go into heaven.

ACTS 1:11 NIV

what really counts

Every Christmas the image of angels singing about the coming of Christ comes to mind. Angels announced the first coming of Christ; they also announced that He would come again. On a hill outside Jerusalem, Jesus did the remarkable. He had spent three years in ministry, traveled from town to town, worked miracles, and gone to the cross. On the cross He died, but on the third day He rose from the dead. He appeared to His followers over the next forty days, but He did what they would never forget. After delivering marching orders to the disciples, Jesus ascended into heaven—bodily.

As the disciples stood with mouths agape, angels appeared and said He would come back in the same way He left. Much has been written about the event that will come, and it's not a new phenomenon. In the New Testament, one in thirty verses deals with the second coming of Jesus. The number of mentions in the Old Testament amounts to well

126

over a thousand verses. For every prophecy regarding the first coming of Christ, there are eight on the Second Coming. In short: It is important and it matters.

This is not just end-of-the-world doom-and-gloom talk. For the believer, the Second Coming is not something to fear but something longed for. We remember Christopher Columbus for his daring trip across the Atlantic and the discovery of the New World. Most people don't know that he predicted the end of the world. In his book *The Book of Prophecy,* Columbus predicted that the world would end no later than 1656. He seems to have been a little off. The date and time of Christ's appearing are not known to us, but the reality of His return is.

The Bible teaches that Jesus will return personally, visibly, in glory and power, with the angels, and unexpectedly. This is great news for the future and power for today. Knowing Christ is coming for His own gives us a sense of belonging and the assurance that He has not forgotten us. Jesus may come before you finish this book. He may not come for decades or even centuries. Knowing this will change the way we see our world, our Savior, and ourselves. When parting from another believer, early Christians used to say, "Maranatha." The word means "Our Lord comes." Living is more exciting knowing that it could be today. So, Maranatha.

The Future
Coming Again

What Matters Most...

◎ Understanding that the future is not purely random, but that the Creator of time is still in charge.

◎ Knowing that Jesus has kept all of His promises and will keep the promise He made to return.

◎ Possessing a positive anticipation for Christ's return. The Second Coming is as good as it gets.

◎ Being ready, knowing that you have settled matters with God through Christ.

◎ Living as if this might be the day of Christ's return. Living with anticipation and making the most of each moment.

What Doesn't Matter...

◎ Not being able to see the future. Some people equate uncertainty with fear. No one can look beyond today.

◎ Doubters. Doubt has never changed anything. Belief changes everything.

◎ Time. What is long for you is short to God.

◎ Your plans. Some people have complained that if Jesus came back today, it would mess up their plans.

◎ Date setters. There are those who claim to know the date when Christ will return. Not one of these people has been or will be right.

Focus Points...

They will see the Son of Man coming in clouds with great power and glory. And then He will send forth the angels, and will gather together His elect from the four winds, from the farthest end of the earth to the farthest end of heaven.
MARK 13:26–27 NASB

I am sure that God, who began the good work within you, will continue his work until it is finally finished on that day when Christ Jesus comes back again.
PHILIPPIANS 1:6 NLT

He who testifies to these things says, "Surely I am coming quickly." Amen. Even so, come, Lord Jesus! The grace of our Lord Jesus Christ be with you all. Amen.
REVELATION 22:20–21 NKJV

He will come again but not to deal with our sins again. This time he will bring salvation to all those who are eagerly waiting for him.
HEBREWS 9:28 NLT

what really counts

Oh, I wish He would come today, so that I could lay my crowns at His feet!

QUEEN VICTORIA

The fact of Jesus' coming is the final and unanswerable proof that God cares.

WILLIAM BARCLAY

The Future
Living the Future in the Present

I have fought the good fight, I have finished the course, I have kept the faith; in
the future there is laid up for me the crown
of righteousness, which the Lord, the righteous Judge, will award to me on that day;
and not only to me, but also to all who
have loved His appearing.

2 TIMOTHY 4:7–8 NASB

what really counts

The future is an uncertain place. No one knows what lies around the corner. We try to hedge our bets. If we can, we buy life insurance and health insurance and invest in a retirement program. There's nothing wrong in that; still, the uncertainty of the future is unsettling. It's easy to worry about the future, and many people do. C. S. Lewis, the great British thinker, wrote, "The next moment is as much beyond our grasp, and as much in God's care, as that a hundred years away. Care for the next minute is just as foolish as care for a day in the next thousand years. In neither can we do anything, in both God is doing everything."

This might seem an easy thing to say, but C. S. Lewis spoke from experience. A confirmed bachelor, he finally mar-
ried in midlife. His love for his wife grew. Not many years later he buried her. Disease had taken her after only a short

time of marriage. Yet despite the pain of loss, despite living in England during World War II and seeing the carnage that war could bring, he remained optimistic about the future. Not because he was confident in himself, not because he had faith in humankind or science or family or society, but because he knew who held the future. Worry changes nothing but the worrier; faith changes everything.

We have today. It might be a good day or a day of bad news, but it is our day and the thing that makes today unique is our view of the future. The apostle Paul was nearing death, but he did so with anticipation, saying that he had fought the good fight, that he had lived as he should, and that the faith that helped him through life would see him into the next life. One of the things he knew—not suspected but *knew*—was that Jesus would grant to him the reward he had earned in this life. We can't imagine the greatness of the future that God has planned for us. The key—the thing that matters most—is discovering God's will and following it. The future is a child born of the present. Knowing what God intends to do—has promised to do—changes our view of the present. The more we know of God's plans, the more our present actions change.

The Future
Living the Future in the Present

What Matters Most...

◎ Seeing that God has a plan for your today and your tomorrow.

◎ Knowing that you may not know what the future holds but that you place your trust in God, who holds the future.

◎ Understanding that the present isn't all there is.

◎ Today gives birth to tomorrow, and the results of decisions you make now will be with you in the future.

◎ Doing all you can with what you have and leaving the rest to God.

What **Doesn't** Matter...

◎ Uncertainty. Everyone has an unpredictable future. Human plans are made and changed. God's plans are forever.

◎ Worry. Tomorrow comes whether you want it to or not, but faith gives you confidence and courage.

◎ Limited knowledge. God seldom reveals His entire plan for a person's life all at once. Act on what you know.

◎ Failed promises of others. Everyone has been let down, but God is faithful in all things. Trust Him.

◎ Death. God's plan for you includes an eternity. Death is merely the closing of the first chapter.

Focus Points...

It is God which worketh in you both to will and to do of his good pleasure.
PHILIPPIANS 2:13 KJV

May he turn our hearts to him, to walk in all his ways and to keep the commands, decrees and regulations he gave our fathers.
1 KINGS 8:58 NIV

We are bound to give thanks to God always for you, brethren beloved by the Lord, because God from the beginning chose you for salvation through sanctification by the Spirit and belief in the truth, to which He called you by our gospel, for the obtaining of the glory of our Lord Jesus Christ.
2 THESSALONIANS 2:13–14 NKJV

I am the Alpha and the Omega, the first and the last, the beginning and the end.
REVELATION 22:13 NASB

God's gifts put man's best dreams to shame.
ELISABETH BARRETT BROWNING

Our heavenly Father never takes anything from his children unless he means to give them something better.
GEORGE MÜLLER

What Matters Most to Me About
The Future

The future is intriguing and may at times be even frightening. In many ways you are a slave to time. The future will arrive without consideration of needs, and you have no way to control it. God, however, does. Give some thought to the following:

⊙ *The Bible is clear about the promised return of Christ. He Himself said He would return. He gave His word that He would. The Bible is also clear that Christ could come at any time. If you knew that He would arrive fifteen minutes from now, how would you feel? Jot down those emotions. Do they show positive anticipation or fear?*

what
really
counts

_____

_____

_____

_____

_____

_____

⊙ *If you were absolutely certain that Jesus would return in the next few years, what would you do differently? How would your life change? Would your priorities change? If so, how would your life be different? List a few thoughts about what would change in you.*

_____

_____

_____

_____

_____

◎ *Apart from what God has revealed, the future is unknown, yet God is in control. Knowing that God has a plan for you and for the rest of the world, how could you effectively dovetail the two together? How does your planning involve God's plan? List a few points of connection.*

_____

_____

_____

_____

_____

_____

_____

◎ *One of the clearest expressions of God's will is from the Old Testament book of Micah: "He has told you, O man, what is good; and what does the LORD require of you but to do justice, to love kindness, and to walk humbly with your God?" (6:8 NASB). Jot down a few ideas about how you could further justice, kindness, and humility.*

_____

_____

_____

_____

_____

_____

_____

"I know the plans I have for you," declares the LORD, "plans to prosper you and not to harm you, plans to give you hope and a future."
JEREMIAH 29:11 NIV

WORSHIP

An Introduction

> O come, let us sing for joy to the LORD, let us shout joyfully to the rock of our salvation. Let us come before His presence with thanksgiving, let us shout joyfully to Him with psalms.
>
> PSALM 95:1–2 NASB

what really counts

One of the greatest pieces of music ever written was penned by George Frideric Handel. At the *Messiah*'s first London performance in March 1743, the audience, including the king, was so moved by the "Hallelujah" chorus that they all stood in unison and remained on their feet until the chorus had ended. More than 250 years later, the tradition remains. That is the power of worship. It is not an isolated affair, not the killing of time on a Sunday morning. Instead it is an encounter with other worshipers and, most of all, with the Almighty. When properly done, worship changes us, putting wind beneath our wings.

Worship is a powerful and yet unusual thing. It is

done in a group but remains one of the most private things we do. Our flesh-and-blood hearts connect with the Spirit of God. We are encouraged, motivated, comforted, moved, convicted, prompted, and educated, all at the same time. Worship is indispensable to living a life before God. As some unknown sage said, "The more a man bows before God, the straighter he stands before men." Worship leads to that kind of strength.

Worship can be done individually, but it reaches its height when done as it was designed to be done, in the company of other believers, in church. Every Christian knows that worship is more than tradition; it is connection and empowerment. Worship opens minds and hearts, your mind and heart.

> Worship is the highest and noblest activity of which man, by the grace of God, is capable.
>
> JOHN STOTT

Worship
Forsake Not

> Let us not give up meeting together, as some are in the habit of doing, but let us encourage one another—and all the more as you see the Day approaching.
>
> HEBREWS 10:25 NIV

what really counts

In 1988 the world's attention was fixed on the life-and-death struggle of three gray whales that had become icebound near Point Barrow, Alaska. Television showed the battered, bloodied whales taking turns breathing through a hole in the ice, a hole that was certain to close in the days ahead. Freedom was five miles away. There they could swim free and surface at will. Rescuers cut new holes through the six-inch-thick ice every twenty yards until they were close enough to the open ocean that a Russian icebreaker could clear a path. One of the three whales disappeared and was assumed dead. The other two, now named Siku and Putu, survived, but only because they received help from creatures they couldn't comprehend.

We all need guidance from above. Every Sunday, millions of Christians make their way to church. Some go as families; some go alone. They gather with others of like faith, and they worship. Others, however, fail to make the time for weekly worship. We live in busy times, and many things demand our attention, but worship should never be pushed to the bottom of the list.

The term *worship* comes from an Old English word *weortscipe,* which became *worthy-ship,* which became our *worship*. Worship is an act whereby we declare our belief that God is worthy of our praise, prayers, attention, and our very lives. Jesus founded only one institution on earth, and it wasn't a business, a government, or a school; it was the church, and at the heart of church is worship. Like the whales that needed help from above to survive, so we also need the intervention of God in our lives.

Worship is the most important thing you do this week, and it has nothing to do with how interesting the preacher is, how good the music is, or how well dressed the other worshipers are. What matters is connecting to God. Worship is about more than receiving a blessing from God; it's about giving a blessing to God. *To bless* means "to make happy," and your act of worship pleases your Creator. In response to that, He blesses you. Worshiping with other believers is an idea born in heaven and practiced on earth. When we worship with others, we bless and are blessed. Worship is the most important thing the church does. It is also the most important thing you do.

Worship
Forsake Not

What Matters Most...

◎ Worship is available. In almost every town, every village, every city, there are churches that focus on worship.

◎ Worship is free. That can't be said for every country.

◎ Worship is for God's benefit. You worship because it pleases Him. He loves to hear from you.

◎ Worship is for your benefit. God rewards those who take time to worship. God blesses you as you bless Him.

◎ Worship is for the benefit of others. There is private worship, but believers worship together to everyone's benefit.

What Doesn't Matter...

◎ Church size. Churches come in different sizes, with memberships of from twenty to thousands. What matters is finding the place you can worship.

◎ The church building. Worship doesn't require a church building. Any place Christians gather is a place of worship.

◎ Time. Time spent in church isn't time lost; it is time invested—an investment that pays many returns.

◎ The common myth that worship has no place in the twenty-first century. Time has no effect on the need to worship.

◎ Your previous view of worship. What matters is correct thinking now.

Focus Points...

Fear the LORD your God, serve him only and take your oaths in his name.
DEUTERONOMY 6:13 NIV

Open to me the gates of righteousness; I shall enter through them, I shall give thanks to the LORD.
PSALM 118:19 NASB

Observe the Sabbath day, to keep it holy, as the LORD your God commanded you.
DEUTERONOMY 5:12 NKJV

Enter his gates with thanksgiving; go into his courts with praise. Give thanks to him and bless his name. For the LORD is good. His unfailing love continues forever, and his faithfulness continues to each generation.
PSALM 100:4–5 NLT

Blessing, and glory, and wisdom, and thanksgiving, and honour, and power, and might, be unto our God for ever and ever. Amen.
REVELATION 7:12 KJV

what really counts

Worship is the highest and noblest activity of which man, by the grace of God, is capable.

JOHN STOTT

We are saved to worship God. All that Christ has done for us in the past and all that He is doing now leads to this one end.

A. W. TOZER

Worship
It's Not About Us

> By him therefore let us offer the sacrifice of praise to God continually, that is, the fruit of our lips giving thanks to his name.
>
> HEBREWS 13:15 KJV

what really counts

A pastor was preparing a message for an upcoming Sunday, and he wanted to use the famous painting *Christ at the Door* by William Holman Hunt as an illustration. He searched the Internet for the image, found it, and began to download a digital picture of the painting. Something went wrong. He didn't receive the whole file. He decided to delete the file and start over. He pressed the Delete key, and the computer, as computers do, asked for verification of the command. On the monitor appeared the question "Are you sure you want to delete Christ?" That gave him pause. Avoiding worship is similar. We may use the time for recreation or work, but we have missed an opportunity to do what God created us to do. Worship is that important.

Worship is a message sent to God by His followers, an act of loving communication where everything else is set aside for a time so our attention can be fully fixed upon God. Too often these days, worship is geared to please the worshiper. In an effort to attract more people to the congregation, churches have begun changing worship style, music, the message, and more. There is no sin in this. It is important to reach out to others, but there is a danger in it. If we are not careful, worship becomes mere entertainment. Worship can be entertaining for the worshiper, but our eyes must never divert from the One we came to worship.

It is important to remember that worship isn't about us, but about the Creator. We benefit from worshiping. We receive uncountable blessings and are strengthened, educated, motivated, bolstered, equipped, and empowered, but those are benefits that come from focusing our attention and praise on God through Jesus Christ. In short, it's not about us; it's about Him. To lose sight of that is to delete God from the process.

Worship is one of the things that really count because it has at its heart a relationship made possible by Jesus Christ. We do not merely "go to church"; we "go to God." God is everywhere; He is not confined to church buildings. In fact, the buildings don't compose the church; the people do. When we worship, we touch the Almighty. Jesus made this great promise: "Where two or three come together in my name, there am I with them" (Matthew 18:20 NIV).

Worship
It's Not About Us

What Matters Most...

◎ Remembering that going to worship is going to God. It is the way God designed the process.

◎ Worship is communicating with the Almighty and nothing less. Songs of praise and prayers are sent His way in worship.

◎ Seeing God as the center of worship. The congregation may sit like an audience, but it is God who is the audience.

◎ Worship is giving. It is the giving of time, of praise, of thanksgiving, of prayer—and of yourself to God.

◎ Regular participation in worship. It is a privilege, an honor, and a command.

What Doesn't Matter...

◎ Your busy schedule. There is always something else to do, but it should never replace worship.

◎ Entertainment. There's nothing wrong with a worship service that is exciting and entertaining, but that is not the goal.

◎ Expectations. It's better to go to worship to hear what God has to say than to hear what you expect.

◎ Feeling good. Worship challenges mind, heart, and soul. Sometimes you are challenged to move out of comfortable spots.

Focus Points...

They, after worshiping Him, returned to Jerusalem with great joy, and were continually in the temple praising God.
LUKE 24:52–53 NASB

Suddenly Jesus met them. "Greetings," he said. They came to him, clasped his feet and worshiped him.
MATTHEW 28:9 NIV

The four and twenty elders fall down before him that sat on the throne, and worship him that liveth for ever and ever, and cast their crowns before the throne, saying, Thou art worthy, O Lord, to receive glory and honour and power: for thou hast created all things, and for thy pleasure they are and were created.
REVELATION 4:10–11 KJV

what really counts

They worshiped together at the Temple each day, met in homes for the Lord's Supper, and shared their meals with great joy and generosity—all the while praising God and enjoying the goodwill of all the people. And each day the Lord added to their group those who were being saved.
ACTS 2:46–47 NLT

God is not moved or impressed with our worship until our hearts are moved and impressed by Him.

KELLY SPARKS

The great thing, and the only thing, is to adore and praise God.

THOMAS MERTON

What Matters Most to Me About
Worship

Worship is essential to the spiritual life, and the spiritual life is essential to life in general. In worship the great elements of praise, prayer, fellowship, learning, and more come together. To worship is to involve yourself in a practice that extends back through time and on into the future.

◉ *For most people, time is in short supply. Work, family, and social obligations can swallow up most of a week and leave little extra time. Consequently, many people cut church out of their lives. It's a mistake. Jot down a few things you can do this week to open time for Sunday worship.*

_____

_____

_____

_____

_____

_____

_____

_____

◉ *Worship is a give-and-give thing. You give praise to God, and He blesses you with love, wisdom, direction, and the wonderful sense that you are His. List a few things for which you are thankful to God.*

_____

_____

_____

_____

_____

_____

what
really
counts

◉ *Finding the right church is more than luck. It requires purposeful searching. Strong Bible teaching, services geared to praise, and a friendly congregation make for the ideal church. List a few items that would make church meaningful for you.*

_____

_____

_____

_____

_____

_____

_____

_____

_____

◉ *Whether you've been to church all your life or you have never been, one thing is true: You get out of church what you put in. Most people who are unhappy with church are unhappy with life in general. List several positive attitudes you can take to church with you this Sunday.*

_____

_____

_____

_____

_____

_____

_____

_____

_____

All the earth will worship You, and will sing praises to You; they will sing praises to Your name.

PSALM 66:4 NASB

THE CHURCH

An Introduction

> This mystery is great; but I am speaking with reference to Christ and the church.
>
> EPHESIANS 5:32 NASB

The church is unique in hundreds of ways. It is a bridge between two worlds. It is the place where Christians go to honor God through worship, to study the Bible, to learn, to fellowship, and to grow.

It has faced crushing persecution without being trampled. It has endured fierce hatred without hating in return. There are no ethnic or gender barriers to being part of the church. It is simultaneously ancient and contemporary. All Christian churches have many things in common while at the same time being different from every other church.

The rich go to church, as do the poor. The educated learn in church, as do those with little or no formal education. It is at church that those in the higher strata of society stand on equal footing with those

148

considered lower class. When presidents go to church, they have no greater standing than the usher. In the first-century church, a slave could be a church leader with his owner in subjection to him. Where could that happen other than the church?

The church is a society of sinners—a gathering of good people trying to be better and bad people trying to be good. It is the place that Jesus founded, loved, and died for. It is the place for every believer. It is there that we learn to be more like Christ, not make Christ more like us. In short, church is for everyone.

> The church is not wood and stone, but the company of people who believe in Christ
>
> Martin Luther

The Church
The Strangest Organization in the World

I also say to you that you are Peter, and upon this rock I will build My church; and the gates of Hades will not over-power it.

MATTHEW 16:18 NASB

what really counts

While conducting a national survey on religious values, a pollster asked a man, "What is your church preference?" Expecting to hear Baptist, Lutheran, Presbyterian, or something similar, he was surprised to hear, "Red brick." People often confuse the church with the building. The church has no walls, although the place where it meets does.

The church is unlike any organization in the world. Consider the following. Jesus Christ, God in the flesh, founded it—not a mere human, not a politician, not an earthly king. The King of kings started it. Its early leaders were largely uneducated men. A few had educations worthy of boasting, but most of the disciples had only the basic education of the day, yet they would turn the world upside down. The church began in a distant land that was under the iron control of another nation, a nation opposed to anything that detracted from Caesar worship. Society ostracized and rejected the church's original members. To become part of the church meant taking on a frightening social stigma, and yet people joined by the thousands. Its Founder came from an obscure little town, preached for only three years, and died a horrible death. The church was born into persecution, yet the more persecution increased, the faster the church grew.

There is no other organization like the church. It is meant to be the home of every Christian. Nowhere in the New Testament can we find a Christian not associated with a church. It should be that way today. Consider what happens in church. First, we come of our own free will. There are no "church police." We attend or we don't. The choice remains forever ours. Second, we participate to whatever degree we feel comfortable. None of the ushers have guns. We sing if we want to, we pray if we want to, and we listen to the message if we want to. Or we can tune all that out. Last, we receive the benefits of friendship, fellowship, education, and worship. All of this goes on Sunday after Sunday. The church is the strangest organization ever, and it continues to change the world two thousand years after it began. Church is not an add-on for the person of faith; it is an integral part of the expression of faith. A church in California has for its motto, "The Sunday place to be." That is true for all of us.

The Church
The Strangest Organization in the World

What Matters Most...

◎ Understanding that church is God's gift to you. You should value and appreciate it.

◎ Church is constructed of people, not bricks. No building defines the church, but two or three gathered believers do.

◎ Church is the "Sunday place to be." That is more than a motto; it is a fact of spiritual life.

◎ The church has one Architect: Jesus Christ. It is the only institution He founded.

◎ Knowing that church is the place you grow and help others grow.

What **Doesn't** Matter...

◎ Location. The church is the church in Africa, Asia, Europe, and everywhere else.

◎ Date. The church of the twenty-first century is like the church of the first century. It exists for the same reason.

◎ Your upbringing. Some are brought up in church; others have never crossed the threshold. It is now that matters.

◎ Human leaders. God calls certain people to lead the local church, but the real Head of the church is Christ.

◎ Questions. If you're new to church life, you have questions. That's a good thing. Church is the place to learn.

Focus Points...

Although I hope to come to you soon, I am writing you these instructions so that, if I am delayed, you will know how people ought to conduct themselves in God's household, which is the church of the living God, the pillar and foundation of the truth.
1 TIMOTHY 3:14–15 NIV

No man can lay a foundation other than the one which is laid, which is Jesus Christ.
1 CORINTHIANS 3:11 NASB

He put all things under His feet, and gave Him to be head over all things to the church, which is His body, the fullness of Him who fills all in all.
EPHESIANS 1:22–23 NKJV

what really counts

Christ is the head of the church, which is his body. He is the first of all who will rise from the dead, so he is first in everything.
COLOSSIANS 1:18 NLT

The church is the only institution supernaturally endowed by God. It is the one institution of which Jesus promised that the gates of hell will not prevail against it.
CHUCK COLSON

It is not the business of the church to adapt Christ to men, but men to Christ.
DOROTHY SAYERS

The Church
Ice Cream and the Church

> I also say to you that you are Peter, and upon this rock I will build My church; and the gates of Hades will not overpower it.
> MATTHEW 16:18 NASB

Many years ago, ice cream came in limited flavors. We could choose between vanilla, chocolate, and strawberry, and for the really adventuresome there was Neapolitan—vanilla, chocolate, and strawberry all in one carton. Now we must choose between chocolate-chip-raspberry-caramel-swirl and brownie-macadamia-nut-vanilla-supreme. Choices are good, as long as we get the basic thing we came for—ice cream. Today we also have more "flavors" of churches than can be listed. There are churches with contemporary services, some with traditional services, and some are "blended." There are even churches that have three or four services each Sunday, and none of them are the same.

What, then, is the right church? How do we choose? Ice cream is ice cream, no matter how many tasty additives we put in it. Church is similar, but there are key things to look for. First, a church's primary function is to bring people to worship God through Jesus Christ. If worship is not central to the church, then it is not a church. Second, a church should help its members grow in their knowledge of faith. Third, it should provide a place of service to God. Also, a church must be centered in the Bible. Christians do not worship the Bible; we worship the One who inspired the Bible. If God has inspired it, we should learn as much as we can.

There are three misconceptions about the church. First is that it is a place for religious people. Strictly speaking, Christianity isn't a religion. Religion is the human effort to reach God; Christianity is God's effort to reach humans. Church is a place for everyone. Some think church is a place, but it isn't. It is a relationship. The word *church* in the New Testament means "called-out ones," that is, those who have been called out of their homes to attend an important meeting. A church is a gathering, no matter where that gathering takes place. Others think the church is full of hypocrites. They have us there. The pizza parlor, ballpark, and workplace are also filled with hypocrites. Church is a people place, and people are imperfect. Church is a spiritual hospital, not a meeting of the self-righteous. Sinners belong in church. The key is to find a church that lets you worship, that teaches you truth from the Bible, and that lets you become the spiritual person you were meant to be.

The Church
Ice Cream and the Church

What Matters Most...

◎ Belonging to a church that promotes the Bible. The Bible is an inspired book meant to guide your life.

◎ Belonging to a church that promotes worship. Worship is God's desire and His due.

◎ Belonging to a church that takes people as they are. There are no perfect people outside or inside the church.

◎ Seeing the church as a spiritual hospital for the wounded, a school to dispel spiritual ignorance, a home for people of faith.

◎ Contributing your time, skills, and presence to make the church a better, stronger, more effective organization.

What Doesn't Matter...

◎ Hypocrites. Yes, there are hypocrites in church just as there are hypocrites everywhere you look.

◎ The world's view of the church. It is God's view that matters and the one to which you should heed.

◎ Previous attendance. The church is open to seekers, searchers, and the sure. Everyone stands before God in the same condition.

◎ Imperfect people. The church was never meant to be a country club; it was designed to be a hospital for spiritual healing.

Focus Points...

Give no offense either to Jews or to Greeks or to the church of God; just as I also please all men in all things, not seeking my own profit but the profit of the many, so that they may be saved.
1 CORINTHIANS 10:32–33 NASB

Whatever you do, work at it with all your heart, as working for the Lord, not for men, since you know that you will receive an inheritance from the Lord as a reward. It is the Lord Christ you are serving.
COLOSSIANS 3:23–24 NIV

Speaking to yourselves in psalms and hymns and spiritual songs, singing and making melody in your heart to the Lord; giving thanks always for all things unto God and the Father in the name of our Lord Jesus Christ.
EPHESIANS 5:19–20 KJV

what really counts

We must cease to think of the Church as a gathering of institutions and organizations, and we must get back to the notion that we are the people of God.

D. M. LLOYD-JONES

The church is her true self only when she exists for humanity.

DIETRICK BONHOEFFER

What Matters Most to Me About
The Church

Church has always been an important aspect for the believer. From New Testament times until now, Christians have been attending, working in, and starting new churches. It is part of Christ's command.

◉ *Church is more than a place or a building. It is an entity created by Christ and loved by Him. It is where He blesses His followers. The church's existence came at a great price: His death. In light of that understanding, write down a short list of why church is important in the world.*

_____

_____

_____

_____

_____

_____

_____

◉ *Church is a people place. Its doors are open to those who have been Christians for decades and those who have never before crossed a church threshold. It is a place for you. List a few things that would make church special to you.*

_____

_____

_____

_____

_____

_____

◎ *"The roof would cave in if I ever went to church," many people have said. So far, it's never happened. That's because church is a place for real people. There are no perfect people in church, but there are people who worship the perfect Christ. Instead of thinking why you shouldn't go to church, write some reasons why you should.*

_____

_____

_____

_____

_____

_____

_____

◎ *Church services today run from traditional to youth-oriented. The music varies, the size varies, and the times of the services vary. There is a place where you can be comfortable. List a few items that would make church meaningful for you.*

_____

_____

_____

_____

_____

_____

_____

Unto the church of God which is at Corinth, to them that are sanctified in Christ Jesus, called to be saints, with all that in every place call upon the name of Jesus Christ our Lord, both theirs and ours.

1 CORINTHIANS 1:2 KJV

THE CHURCH

159

WISDOM

An Introduction

> To those called by God to salvation, both Jews and Gentiles, Christ is the mighty power of God and the wonderful wisdom of God.
>
> 1 CORINTHIANS 1:24 NLT

what really counts

In the Old Testament book of Proverbs, the wisest man ever to have lived described wisdom as a woman crying out for notice. Solomon said there are those who pay attention to wisdom and those who ignore it. Wisdom is a skill of the mind, of the heart, and of the soul. No one ever complains about someone being "too wise."

The opposite of wisdom is foolishness. Foolishness is the willful ignoring of truth. It is seldom chosen, but many people default to that way of thinking. God wants us to be wise, and not with just any kind of wisdom but with a wisdom that comes directly from Him. And who can know more about wisdom than God Himself?

Wisdom, the Bible tells us, is more valuable than rubies and gold. In the twenty-first century there isn't much talk of wisdom. Our world is filled with more wise guys than wise people. Wisdom changes not only what we do, but who we are. A world seen through wise eyes looks very different from that seen without wisdom.

During the 1960s and 1970s there was a great interest in psychic ability, sometimes called a sixth sense. Researchers wondered if humans didn't have more senses than the obvious five: smell, sight, hearing, touch, and taste. Wisdom is that sixth sense. It is the ability to see with spiritual eyes and recognize truth. Solomon asked for wisdom over riches, and God gave him far more than the king expected. Wisdom is worth asking for.

> The truly wise are those whose souls are in Christ.
> SAINT AMBROSE

Wisdom
In the Know

> If any of you needs wisdom, you should ask God for it. He is generous and enjoys giving to all people, so he will give you wisdom.
>
> JAMES 1:5 NCV

what really counts

"Wisdom," someone said, "is the quality that keeps you from getting into situations where you need it." There are many definitions of *wisdom*, and none of them quite seem to say it all. One English dictionary defines *wisdom* as (1) "good sense," (2) "accumulated learning," (3) "opinion widely held," and (4) "ancient teachings and sayings." In the general sense this is true, but in the spiritual sense wisdom is much more. Wisdom is more than knowledge. Knowledge can be memorized, analyzed, and even codified. Wisdom knows what to do with knowledge. It is something that enables us to see what is right and to do it. Biblical wisdom is more than good sense. It is the comprehension of what is seen with spiritual insight. It is the "God point of view" where we see through His eyes.

John Maxwell tells of a sailor stationed in Pearl Harbor in 1941. On December 7, Japanese aircraft attacked the naval base, and this man took his position at one of the ship's guns.

He fired round after round at the attacking planes, but none went down. That's when it occurred to him that his ship was prepped for naval exercises but not for real battle. He was firing blanks. To look at him standing on deck, machine gun blazing, it would appear that he was doing battle, but the truth was, he lacked the important tools to do the job. Wisdom is the empowerment that God gives us so we can do what needs to be done.

Wisdom comes from God, and that wisdom is different from that found in the world. God's wisdom puts us in the know about life, work, family, service, and the future. Wisdom is the ability to see the world and our lives from the point of view of God, to see a bigger picture that elevates us in our motivation and action.

Wisdom teeth are those molars that appear when we are about twenty-one years old. People call them wisdom teeth because they arrive as we approach adulthood, a time when we are supposed to be wiser than in the days of our youth. Spiritual wisdom isn't a function of age or even experience, although both help. Spiritual wisdom is a gift from God, and God gives it to whoever cares enough to ask. Ask for wisdom, and ask for it again tomorrow and the next day, and God will give it. Those who ask, receive.

Wisdom
In the Know

What Matters Most...

◎ Seeing wisdom as different from knowledge. Knowledge is good; wisdom is mandatory.

◎ Understanding that wisdom is seeing your life and the world from God's point of view. "God-sight" is insight.

◎ Some wisdom is earned through experience, but spiritual wisdom comes from God as a gift.

◎ Remembering that God desires to give wisdom and that He gives to all who ask Him for it.

◎ Using wisdom for the glory of God, the benefit of self, and the betterment of others.

What Doesn't Matter...

◎ A wiseacre is not the same as a wise man or woman. Being wise isn't about being a know-it-all; it's about seeing everything the way God sees it and knowing what to do.

◎ The world has a type of wisdom, but it is a pale thing compared to the wisdom that comes from above.

◎ Wisdom has a purpose—not a desire to be praised, but a hunger to do what is right.

◎ Unwise mistakes. Everyone has made them, but that does not disqualify anyone from receiving God's wisdom today.

Focus Points...

The mouth of the righteous utters wisdom, and his tongue speaks justice. The law of his God is in his heart; his steps do not slip.
PSALM 37:30–31 NASB

Surely you desire truth in the inner parts; you teach me wisdom in the inmost place.
PSALM 51:6 NIV

The LORD gives wisdom; from His mouth come knowledge and understanding; He stores up sound wisdom for the upright; He is a shield to those who walk uprightly.
PROVERBS 2:6–7 NKJV

Be careful how you live, not as fools but as those who are wise. Make the most of every opportunity for doing good in these evil days.
EPHESIANS 5:15–16 NLT

what really counts

You can't access wisdom by the megabyte. Wisdom is concerned with how we relate to people, to the world, and to God.

EDMUND P. CLOWNEY

Knowledge is the power of the mind, wisdom is the power of the soul.

JULIE SHANNAHAN

165

Wisdom
The Mind of Christ

Let this mind be in you which was also in Christ Jesus.

PHILIPPIANS 2:5 NKJV

what really counts

In the early days of computers, programmers coined the term *GIGO*. It stood for, "garbage in, garbage out." They were saying that a computer was only as good as the program it was asked to run. Human beings aren't much different. What we put into our minds usually comes out in our words and actions. People say, "You are what you eat." More to the point, "You are what you think." It is a simple statement, but one with profound ramifications. Your thoughts affect your spiritual health.

Physicians and psychologists tell us that mental attitude is the single most important factor concerning our physical health and emotional happiness. Mental attitude is a factor in 90 percent of illnesses. Negative and bitter people get sick more often and more severely. What we allow into our brains impacts all that we do, say, and feel. We are the guardians of what enters our brains. Strangely, most people are fussier about what enters their bodies than what enters their minds. What enters the body leaves; what enters the mind stays.

The apostle Paul wrote to a church in the ancient city of Philippi, "Let this mind be in you which was also in Christ Jesus." We miss something in the English translation of the verse. In the original biblical language, the words come as a command, not a suggestion. Paul isn't saying that this is a nice way of doing things; he states that it is the right way, the Christian way. There's something else in this verse—choice. We get to choose this course of action. We can choose to have the same mind as Christ.

Some estimate our minds hold one hundred trillion thoughts. We police those thoughts. In AD 79 Mount Vesuvius destroyed the city of Pompeii and left the remains of buildings and the three-dimensional forms of the people who died there. The bodies formed molds for the falling ash that hardened, leaving exact representations of the deceased. Researchers discovered a Roman sentinel perfectly preserved at his post. As others fled for safety, he stood his ground. In the face of death he refused to leave his post. One thousand years later, he was discovered still standing guard. Our minds need such faithful guards who let in that which is good, productive, beneficial, and godly, and keep out the poisons that so often afflict the world. Choose the mind of Christ.

Wisdom
The Mind of Christ

What Matters Most...

⦿ Knowing that your thoughts affect your spiritual life and your life in general.

⦿ The great gift of choice works in your mind. You choose what you will read, see, hear, and think.

⦿ You are what you think. Those things that you dwell upon become a part of your daily thoughts and actions.

⦿ You can have the mind of Christ, His attitude, His thought processes, His values. Like many things, that is a choice.

⦿ Disciplined thinking requires prayer and practice. The more you do it, the better you become.

What Doesn't Matter...

⦿ An open mind. Some consider an open mind a virtue, but there is a reason to close doors.

⦿ Wayward thoughts. Everyone has them, but you don't have to invite them to stay. You choose which thoughts move in and stay.

⦿ Not everything said, sung, acted, discussed, printed, or announced is true or beneficial, just as not everything edible is food.

⦿ Believing everything that is said. God gave you a mind for a reason and a reason to have a mind.

Focus Points...

I will bless the LORD who has counseled me; indeed, my mind instructs me in the night. I have set the LORD continually before me; because He is at my right hand, I will not be shaken.
PSALM 16:7–8 NASB

The mind of sinful man is death, but the mind controlled by the Spirit is life and peace; the sinful mind is hostile to God. It does not submit to God's law, nor can it do so.
ROMANS 8:6–7 NIV

"Who has known the mind of the LORD that he may instruct Him?" But we have the mind of Christ.
1 CORINTHIANS 2:16 NKJV

There must be a spiritual renewal of your thoughts and attitudes. You must display a new nature because you are a new person, created in God's likeness—righteous, holy, and true.
EPHESIANS 4:23–24 NLT

what really counts

A Christian is a person who thinks in believing and believes in thinking.
SAINT AUGUSTINE OF HIPPO

Change your thoughts and you change your world.
NORMAN VINCENT PEALE

169

What Matters Most to Me About
Wisdom

Life requires good thinking, sound opinions, and tons of wisdom. The human mind is an amazing thing as it reflects how great is the Creator, but each person is responsible for his decisions and thoughts. You need wisdom and the mind of Christ.

◉ *Some wisdom is earned. You gain it simply by living and making mistakes. Godly wisdom is a gift from God. Some people are wise in some areas and not so wise in others. Jot down a few areas of your life where you could use more wisdom, and then make it a matter of prayer.*

what
really
counts

_____

_____

_____

_____

_____

_____

◉ *Wisdom is not only for your benefit. Some of the events in your life—good and bad—have prepared you to help others. Write down a few experiences you've had that have made you wiser and that could help someone else.*

_____

_____

_____

_____

_____

_____

◉ *Every day, you are bombarded with images, music, and words, and each one takes up a few brain cells. There they stay for most of your life. You are the guardian of your mind. List three or four things you want to have in your mind (don't forget the spiritual) and a few things you don't.*

_____

_____

_____

_____

_____

_____

_____

_____

◉ *One of the most powerful things in life is prayer. Prayer in your mind brings out the best of your thinking. All people struggle with thoughts they wish they didn't have and thoughts they wish they had more often. Write a few down, then make them a matter of prayer.*

_____

_____

_____

_____

_____

_____

_____

_____

We have received, not the spirit of the world, but the Spirit who is from God, that we might know the things that have been freely given to us by God.

1 CORINTHIANS 2:12 NKJV

TRUST

An Introduction

> He who dwells in the shelter of the Most High will abide in the shadow of the Almighty. I will say to the LORD, "My refuge and my fortress, my God, in whom I trust!"
>
> PSALM 91:1–2 NASB

what really counts

Trust is a precious thing. It is especially precious for those who have been betrayed by someone they trusted. In our world, such things are not odd. Everyone, sooner or later, is let down by a friend, a fellow worker, even a family member. The natural response is to stop trusting. Believers, however, don't operate in the natural way; they operate in the supernatural.

There remains One who is completely and fully trustworthy. We all need someone like that. Even General Dwight D. Eisenhower, who gained fame for his role in World War II and for his popular presidency, said, "This is what I found out about religion: it gives you courage to make the decision you must make in a crisis and the confidence to leave the results to a higher Power. Only by trust in God can a man carrying responsibility find repose."

We all have responsibilities. Some more than others, but each bears a load, and there are times when we need to place our trust in others. And, of course, there are times when we must place our trust in God. The sad thing is, so many people wait for a crisis to do what could be done daily—placing confidence in God. God is trustworthy in the big things and the little things, and we can count on Him at all times.

Every day is chock-full of choices and challenges, but you can make every day better by having the courage to trust the One who is always trustworthy.

Trust the past to God's mercy, the present to his love, and the future to his providence.
SAINT AUGUSTINE OF HIPPO

Trust

The Power of Trust

> Trust in the LORD with all your heart and do not lean on your own understanding. In all your ways acknowledge Him, and He will make your paths straight.
>
> PROVERBS 3:5–6 NASB

what really counts

The verses closest to the center of the protestant Bible are Psalm 118:8–9: "It is better to trust in the LORD than to put confidence in man. It is better to trust in the LORD than to put confidence in princes" (NKJV). Just as these verses are centered in the Bible, so should they be centered in our hearts. Ours is not a trusting world, and many people find trusting a challenge. Yet the Bible tells us, "Trust in the LORD with all your heart" (Proverbs 3:5 NIV). How do we do that? How, in uncertain times, can we learn to trust God?

A radio announcer once asked New York Giants manager Leo Durocher, "Barring the unforeseen, Leo, will your club get the pennant?" Durocher shot back, "There ain't gonna be no unforeseen." Our world teaches otherwise. Family members hurt us, disease seems to come from nowhere, accidents happen, financial reversals surprise us, and we are left with the feeling that there is nothing certain in life. God is certain.

In fact, He may be the only thing certain in the universe. Life is hard—at times disappointing, difficult, and even depressing—but God remains on His throne. Seeing that changes our perspective and replaces the negative feelings with confidence and hope.

There's power in trusting God. A man took some time out of his day to watch a Little League game. He arrived a little late, so he asked one of the young players what the score was. "It's 18–0; we're losing." The man felt bad for the boy. "Well, at least you're not discouraged." That puzzled the boy. "Discouraged? We're not discouraged. We haven't been up to bat yet." Sometimes we despair even before we've given God a chance at bat.

God has never promised us an easy life. Christians are not exempt from trouble; they are empowered in trouble. People of faith experience the same frustrations and disappointments as other people, but they do so with their trust firmly placed in God—and that changes the way they endure difficulty. Trust can never be demanded; it must be given. Our ability to trust says something about us as well as the One we trust. God calls on us to place our trust in Him. Trusting is not the same as knowledge. Often we are left with questions about why something happened, but one thing we need never question is God's trustworthiness. God says, "Trust Me."

Trust
The Power of Trust

What Matters Most...

◎ Certainty in uncertainty. Life can keep you off balance, but God-centered attention keeps you from losing your footing.

◎ Trustworthiness is a rare commodity in the world, but God is trustworthy in every way.

◎ The future may be uncertain, but He who holds the future is certain in all things.

◎ Giving God a chance. Too often you surrender before utilizing your greatest strength—your God.

◎ God can change your situation or your view of your situation. Either way, things are better.

What Doesn't Matter...

◎ Disappointment in others. You've been let down before. Still, the untrustworthiness of others doesn't eclipse the trustworthiness of God.

◎ Uncertainty. It's uncomfortable and it's real, but it doesn't really count. You can trust God.

◎ Pride. "I can do it all by myself" doesn't count. Life isn't an issue of pride, but one of a God-pleasing life.

◎ Feelings. Emotions are deceiving. Trust is setting your situation in the hands of God and responding to His direction.

Focus Points...

Those who know Your name will put their trust in You, for You, O Lord, have not forsaken those who seek You.
PSALM 9:10 NASB

Trust in the Lord and do good; dwell in the land and enjoy safe pasture. Delight yourself in the Lord and he will give you the desires of your heart.
PSALM 37:3–4 NIV

Blessed is the man who trusts in the Lord, and whose hope is the Lord. For he shall be like a tree planted by the waters, which spreads out its roots by the river, and will not fear when heat comes; but its leaf will be green, and will not be anxious in the year of drought, nor will cease from yielding fruit.
JEREMIAH 17:7–8 NKJV

what really counts

We should be to the praise of his glory, who first trusted in Christ. In whom ye also trusted, after that ye heard the word of truth, the gospel of your salvation: in whom also after that ye believed, ye were sealed with that holy Spirit of promise.
EPHESIANS 1:12–13 KJV

There is no other method of living piously and justly, than that of depending upon God.

JOHN CALVIN

He who trusts in himself is lost. He who trusts in God can do all things.

SAINT ALPHONSUS LIGUORI

Trust
The Resting Place of Faith

> Do not let your heart be troubled; believe in God, believe also in Me.
>
> JOHN 14:1 NASB

what really counts

One of the first things a student pilot learns is to trust his instruments more than his own senses. As one instructor said, "You must learn that even though you may feel you are flying south, if your compass says you're flying east, you'd better believe it." Faith is like that. At times we feel conflicted, uncertain, and confused, and we need a compass to direct us. That compass is Jesus. He is the One in whom we place our trust and faith. Faith always has an object. Some people trust in law, some people trust in themselves, and some people can't trust at all. Faith has a resting place, and knowing where that is really counts.

Our greatest purpose is also our greatest strength: faith in Jesus. Life can be uncertain, but Jesus is always true. San Francisco has a reputation for steep and sometimes treacherous roads. Three such streets, Filbert Street, Russian Hill, and Twenty-second Street, have made the *Guinness Book of World*

Records. Lombard Street made the list too. It is the most crooked road in the world. It has eight consecutive ninety-degree turns, and each turn has only a twenty-foot radius. Driving down that steep, winding road can be unnerving. Just like life. We face twists and turns. Some we expect, and others catch us off guard. If we stay with the One who called Himself "the Way," we will complete the course.

Contrary to popular belief, faith isn't held; it's placed. Faith describes our response to the facts of belief. It is us putting our eternal lives in the hands of Jesus, who died to give us that eternal life. Faith needs exercise. The more we pursue our spiritual purpose, the stronger our faith becomes. This is not an occasional thing, but a life choice.

Some time ago, a man took an American Indian blanket to the *Antiques Roadshow,* a television program where people bring antique items for experts to examine. The appraiser studied the blanket and then asked the owner, "Are you a wealthy man?" The owner assured him he was not. After describing the details of the chief's blanket, he announced its value at $250,000. The owner was stunned and said, "And to think, I've been hanging it over the back of my sofa for years." He didn't know what he had. We need to know what we have in faith. We have everything.

Trust
The Resting Place of Faith

What Matters Most...

◎ Knowing that faith isn't held; rather, it's placed. It is not simple belief, but belief that has been acted upon.

◎ God is your compass, and His Word is your map. No matter what you face, you know that He won't change.

◎ Jesus is "the way, the truth, and the life." He is all those things and remains all those things.

◎ God turns inner conflict into inner peace, confusion into certainty, and doubt into trust.

◎ When you have faith you are wealthy. Nothing else in your life has power or is valuable.

What **Doesn't** Matter...

◎ The winding roads of life. Every life has twists and turns. No matter how crooked the road, God's path remains straight.

◎ Knowing about faith, understanding faith, or talking about faith. Until faith is placed in God, it is nothing more than a concept.

◎ All the wrong roads in your past. No matter where you are, you can get back on track.

◎ Philosophies. The one idea that makes a real difference is knowing that God loves you.

◎ Years of wasted effort. At any moment, applied belief in Christ changes an eternal future.

Focus Points...

By awesome deeds You answer us in righteousness, O God of our salvation, You who are the trust of all the ends of the earth and of the farthest sea.
PSALM 65:5 NASB

Turn to me and be saved, all you ends of the earth; for I am God, and there is no other.
ISAIAH 45:22 NIV

Blessed be the Lord, who daily loads us with benefits, the God of our salvation!
PSALM 68:19 NKJV

Jesus said, "Come to me, all of you who are weary and carry heavy burdens, and I will give you rest. Take my yoke upon you. Let me teach you, because I am humble and gentle, and you will find rest for your souls."
MATTHEW 11:28–29 NLT

what really counts

Thus saith the LORD, thy Redeemer, the Holy One of Israel; I am the LORD thy God which teacheth thee to profit, which leadeth thee by the way that thou shouldest go.
ISAIAH 48:17 KJV

The point of having an open mind, like having an open mouth, is to close it on something solid.

G. K. CHESTERTON

Faith is kept alive in us, and gathers strength, more from practice than from speculations.

JOSEPH ADDISON

What Matters Most to Me About
Trust

Purpose revolves around faith and trust. Those two qualities put life in perspective. Yet the world turns many people into untrusting cynics. To walk with God, you must trust Him with your present and future life. That means handing over your trust and faith to Him. Then, and only then, can you live on purpose.

◎ *Trust requires being open and transparent before God. Since He knows all things, this should not be difficult, but still people hesitate to be honest with Him. Maybe because being honest with God means being honest with oneself. What is on your heart and mind that you need to turn over to God?*

_____

_____

_____

_____

_____

◎ *Trust is the release of responsibility, but it is an involving of God in your life. God doesn't accept part-time work. You cannot trust Him with one concern and keep others for yourself; you cannot ask Him to help in one area of your life but lock Him out of the rest. Jot down a few areas in your life you're reluctant to trust God with, and then turn them over to Him.*

_____

_____

_____

_____

◎ *Faith is something you have. Faith is something you hand over to God. Faith has a direction and a destination. Faith is not mere belief; it is belief that is placed in God. Faith is trust in daily life, and it includes work, family, recreation, rest, and every other area of existence. Write, "I will trust God for _____" and fill in the blank.*

_____

_____

_____

_____

_____

_____

_____

◎ *Jesus described Himself as the "Way," the path that believers follow. That means that as a disciple of His, you follow the course He has set. The course you set is often a different direction. What areas of your life have been off course? List them and then determine to change directions.*

_____

_____

_____

_____

_____

_____

_____

_____

You have been my hope, O Sovereign LORD, my confidence since my youth.
PSALM 71:5 NIV

PEACE

An Introduction

> After eight days His disciples were again inside, and Thomas with them. Jesus came, the doors having been shut, and stood in their midst and said, "Peace be with you."
>
> JOHN 20:26 NASB

what really counts

"We came in peace for all mankind." That was the motto for *Apollo 11*. On the moon rests a plaque with those words. The Sea of Tranquility is the home for that plaque, and it is likely to stay undisturbed there for longer than we can imagine. Neil Armstrong and Buzz Aldrin, as emissaries from earth, left a message of peace. Peace has been on the mind of humankind from the beginning, but it remains an elusive dream.

Perhaps there is so little peace on earth because there is so little peace in our hearts. Peace is tranquillity in the midst of a storm. Once Jesus was in a fishing boat with His disciples. A terrible storm arose, and the frightened disciples turned to Jesus for help. To their amazement then and our astonishment now, Jesus was fast asleep. How does one sleep in a storm-tossed boat? The disciples pleaded for help, and Jesus quieted the storm with His words.

When life rages, Jesus grants peace. As the disciples discovered, they couldn't find peace in their efforts, in their wishing, or in their skills. They found peace by turning their faces from the storm and looking at the unbothered Savior. He was the perfect image of peace; He was the One who brought peace to the storm, and He remains the Author of our peace.

Peace is not elusive; it is not hidden from our sight. It's a prayer away. Happiness is learned. Living in and with peace takes practice, but the Source of peace is ever present.

> Even if I knew that tomorrow the world would go to pieces, I would still plant my apple tree.
> MARTIN LUTHER

Peace
Just What You Need

Peace I leave with you; My peace I give to you; not as the world gives do I give to you. Do not let your heart be troubled, nor let it be fearful.

JOHN 14:27 NASB

what really counts

Alfred Bernhard Nobel has a famous name. Every year, large cash prizes are given to individuals whose achievements in chemistry, physics, medicine, literature, and world peace have made the world a better place to live. In his will, he stipulated that most of his large estate be set aside and the interest from those monies be shared with the winners. The Nobel Prize is the most prestigious award in the world. This is especially true for the Nobel Peace Prize. Here's the irony: The nineteenth-century Swedish chemist made his fortune working with his father in developing mines, torpedoes, and other explosives. He is the inventor of dynamite. Still, this maker of weapons had a head and a heart for peace.

Peace is an elusive possession. We are hungry for personal peace. More than fifty years ago, evangelist Billy Graham said in his book *Peace with God,* "I know men who would write a check for a million dollars if they could find peace." The need for peace is everywhere. The average American marriage lasts 9.4 years; half of all marriages end in divorce; more than 1 million children run away from home every year; every two minutes a child is molested. The ugly list goes on.

Everyone has a need for peace, but few understand it. Peace is not happiness. Peace is not joy. Peace is not rejoicing. Yet peace can yield all those things. The Hebrew word is *shalom,* and it means "completeness," "health," and, of course, "peace." It appears 237 times in the Old Testament. The New Testament Greek word is *eirene,* and it means "national harmony," "tranquillity," and "freedom from conflict." It is used about 92 times in the New Testament and is found in every book except 1 John.

Spiritual peace dwells within but comes from without. The peace that "passes understanding" is God-sent, and no other source for it exists. Jesus gives the peace we need. His promise was that He would leave peace with us. He said, "Peace I send to you." The peace we need is personally given by Christ. It isn't the kind of peace you discover on your own or that you find in the world. The world knows nothing of peace. There have been approximately 150 conflicts between nations since World War II. Peace has a source: Jesus. Peace has a destination: our hearts. There's a reason Jesus is called the Prince of Peace.

Peace
Just What You Need

What Matters Most...

- ◎ *Peace* is more than a word, more than a concept, more than a hope. It's a reality for those in Christ.

- ◎ You feel peace inwardly, but it comes from an outside Source. Jesus brings peace, gives peace, and heightens peace.

- ◎ Peace is often felt when its counterpart is swirling around you. In difficulty and uncertainty, you experience peace.

- ◎ The peace Jesus gives surpasses your ability to describe and understand. It is beyond explanation.

- ◎ Peace is possible, peace is real, and it can be yours.

What **Doesn't** Matter...

- ◎ Turmoil. It comes to every life, but the peace of Christ is not disturbed by its noisy surroundings of difficulty.

- ◎ A peaceful world. As good an ideal as that is, the spiritual peace goes beyond earthly peace.

- ◎ Absence of conflict. Peace is more than the absence of conflict; it is a spiritual comfort in all situations. Such peace liberates from within.

- ◎ Peace with self and peace with others. These are blessings, but peace with God is so much more. It is life-changing.

- ◎ Finding peace. Peace isn't found; it is given.

Focus Points...

In peace I will both lie down and sleep, for You alone, O Lord, make me to dwell in safety.
Psalm 4:8 NASB

To us a child is born, to us a son is given, and the government will be on his shoulders. And he will be called Wonderful Counselor, Mighty God, Everlasting Father, Prince of Peace.
Isaiah 9:6 NIV

Peace I leave with you, My peace I give to you; not as the world gives do I give to you. Let not your heart be troubled, neither let it be afraid.
John 14:27 NKJV

Since we have been made right in God's sight by faith, we have peace with God because of what Jesus Christ our Lord has done for us.
Romans 5:1 NLT

what really counts

Keep your heart in peace; let nothing in this world disturb it; everything has an end.

Saint John of the Cross

If God be our God, He will give us peace in trouble. When there is a storm without, He will make peace within. The world can create trouble in peace, but God can create peace in trouble.

Thomas Watson

189

Peace
Burden-Tossing

Cast all your anxiety on him
because he cares for you.

1 PETER 5:7 NIV

One of the strangest sports to witness is the Scottish caber toss. This unusual sport requires a man to lift and hold a caber, a wood pole twenty feet long and weighing 120 pounds, then toss it so that it flies end over end. Men have been doing this since the sixteenth century. If only we could toss our burdens off the same way. No one goes through life free of trouble. Concerns, pains, doubts, anxiety, rejection, and more come our way, and some stay. Such burdens leech the joy of living out of us, and no one is exempt.

A story is told of the emperor Augustus, a man with the weight of a kingdom on his shoulders. Augustus heard that a man who was heavily in debt lived in Rome, yet despite his financial woes, he slept peacefully. So impressed was Augustus that he offered to buy the man's bed. It would have been a useless purchase. No bed can ease a person's burdens, but Jesus can. It was the apostle Peter who wrote to the persecuted Christians in his day and advised them to "cast all your anxiety on him because he cares for you" (1 Peter 5:7 NIV). He advised burden-tossing.

Simple as it sounds, many people struggle with letting go of their problems. Instead of releasing their burdens, they cling to them as if they have become old friends. Three pastors went hiking up a mountain. One was a fit senior. The other two were younger by two decades. Halfway up the slope it became clear that the first ones to the top would not be the two young men. One had fallen well behind. The older pastor descended the grade until he reached his friend who was struggling under the weight of his backpack. "Give me your pack," the senior pastor said. "No," the young man replied. "You have your own to carry." The older man frowned. Finally he said, "Humble yourself, brother. Give me your pack." He did.

Pride keeps many people from turning to Christ for help. "I can do it all myself," they say. Perhaps they can, but they miss the joy of sharing the journey of life with Christ. It isn't a weakness to accept help any more than it is to offer it; it is wisdom. The Bible says to toss our burdens, anxieties, and worries onto Christ. It's time to start tossing.

Peace
Burden-Tossing

What Matters Most...

◉ Believing that God wants you to toss your burdens on Him. Those whom God loves cannot inconvenience Him.

◉ Understanding that burden-tossing is a choice like so many other spiritual strengths. You can bear them or release them.

◉ God empowers you in problems, encourages you in difficulty, and guides you in confusion.

◉ Releasing your concerns is a matter of faith, trust, and belief. It is an act of courage. One that God rewards.

What **Doesn't** Matter...

◉ Worry. Living with worry is counterproductive. Acknowledge your worries, then give them to God.

◉ Anxiety. Anxiety is apprehension come to live with us. It is concern about the future. Anxiety has never helped anyone. Toss it.

◉ Burdens. Burdens sit heavy on our emotional shoulders, weighing us down. God can take those burdens off your shoulders.

◉ Inactivity. Tossing our burdens is not an excuse to avoid responsibility, but it does free us to do what needs to be done.

Focus Points...

I would have despaired unless I had believed that I would see the goodness of the Lord in the land of the living. Wait for the Lord; be strong and let your heart take courage; yes, wait for the Lord.
PSALM 27:13–14 NASB

I say to you, do not worry about your life, what you will eat or what you will drink; nor about your body, what you will put on. Is not life more than food and the body more than clothing?
MATTHEW 6:25 NKJV

Be anxious for nothing, but in everything by prayer and supplication, with thanksgiving, let your requests be made known to God; and the peace of God, which surpasses all understanding, will guard your hearts and minds through Christ Jesus.
PHILIPPIANS 4:6–7 NKJV

what really counts

Who among you fears the Lord and obeys his servant? If you are walking in darkness, without a ray of light, trust in the Lord and rely on your God.
ISAIAH 50:10 NLT

Don't talk to others about your problem, speak to the problem about your God!
CARL-GUSTAF SEVERIN

By casting our burdens upon Him, our spirits become light and cheerful; we are freed from a thousand anxieties.
JOHN NEWTON

193

What Matters Most to Me About
Peace

Happiness is an elusive quality. If it could be bottled and sold, it would make millions. Peace is not in pills but in a person, Jesus Christ, and that peace is available to people of faith. In the chaos that sometimes comes to life, learning to accept the peace that passes understanding is the wisest action you can take.

◎ *Peace is possible. That's hard to believe for some who have been through tough times. It is, however, true. But real peace and happiness can come only through Christ, who fulfills every area of life. In what areas of your life would you most like a sense of peace?*

what
really
counts

_____
_____
_____
_____
_____
_____

◎ *Jesus is the Prince of Peace. It is He who brings the sense that all is well even in the midst of the greatest turmoil. It is in turmoil that peace is felt. Write, "Lord, I need peace in _____," then give it to God through prayer. Keep praying over the list.*

_____
_____
_____
_____
_____
_____

Everyone has burdens. No one likes them, but few do anything about them. The Bible teaches that you have the choice and the opportunity to cast your anxiety upon God. It is an act of love on your part to do so; it is an act of love on His part to take those burdens. What should you be casting upon God?

_____

_____

_____

_____

_____

_____

_____

_____

Tossing your burdens on God does not remove your responsibility to be part of God's solution. Using the list you just made, write down a few things you can do to make the situation better.

_____

_____

_____

_____

_____

_____

_____

_____

In my distress I called upon the LORD, and cried to my God for help; He heard my voice out of His temple, and my cry for help before Him came into His ears.

PSALM 18:6 NASB

CHARACTER

An Introduction

> Do not be misled: "Bad company corrupts good character."
>
> 1 CORINTHIANS 15:33 NIV

what really counts

Henry Ward Beecher said, "He is rich or poor according to what he is, not according to what he has." Our character is the real us. Speaking more loudly than clothing, possessions, or even words we may utter, character reveals the inner us. More than anything else, people judge us by the character we put forth.

Character possesses many attributes. Our emotions play a part, our words say more than the terms themselves, and our actions reflect our inner spirit. No one quality defines our character. It is what we are and what we do; it is what we think and what we say; it is the private thoughts and the public opinions. Sometimes the world sees us differently from how we see ourselves.

CHARACTER

It is good to have an objective opinion, an opinion that counts. God is a good judge of character. But He sees differently than we do. God told the prophet Samuel, "God sees not as man sees, for man looks at the outward appearance, but the LORD looks at the heart" (1 Samuel 16:7 NASB). God judges with different criteria. His scorecard looks like no other. God looks at your heart, not at what you wear or where you work. God doesn't look at your résumé.

Your character counts, not only to you, not only to others, but to God. Developing a solid, spiritual character is among the highest of goals. Discipline, honesty, listening to the right advice, and many things more are the facets that make our character shine, that give us a character that pleases God and ourselves.

Of all the properties which belong to honorable men, not one is so highly prized as that of character.

HENRY CLAY

Character
Heeding the Right Advice

> This book of the law shall not depart from your mouth, but you shall meditate on it day and night, so that you may be careful to do according to all that is written in it; for then you will make your way prosperous, and then you will have success.
>
> JOSHUA 1:8 NASB

what really counts

Years ago a popular television commercial appeared. It was for the brokerage firm of E. F. Hutton. The commercials had one of the most memorable taglines in the industry, "When E. F. Hutton speaks, people listen." This was reinforced in the ads when someone in a crowded room began a conversation saying, "My broker is E. F. Hutton, and E. F. Hutton says—" Everyone in the crowd would stop what they were doing to eavesdrop on the free advice. Years later the firm would be in legal trouble with about two thousand criminal counts against them. The firm of E. F. Hutton is no more. Advice is good if it is the right advice. Advice is cheap; truth takes a little work.

Where do we get our advice for life? The Bible and prayer. The Bible is God's inspired Word, and prayer is conversation with God. A. W. Tozer told of an elderly believer who was asked, "Which is more important: reading God's Word or praying?" The experienced believer replied, "Which is more important to a bird, the right wing or the left?" Bible study and prayer go hand in hand, and so does seeking counsel.

Sir Edmund Hillary reached the top of Mount Everest in 1953. He was knighted for his achievement, and his name was put down in the history books. Often overlooked is Tenzing Norgay, the Sherpa guide who was standing alongside Hillary. Norgay provided needed advice, and Sir Edmund was wise to heed it. Before us is the uncharted course of our lives, and heeding advice is wise. There are many Christians who have deep biblical understanding, life experience, and learning that can provide wise counsel. It makes sense to take good advice from the right people.

Few men stand with the stature of Moses. Moses was reared in the court of a king and chosen to lead to freedom the captive children of Israel. He saw miracle after miracle performed by God through him, and he brought the Israelites to the edge of the Promised Land. His résumé would intimidate anyone, and yet when the burden of the work became too much, he took advice from his father-in-law, Jethro, to delegate authority. Moses needed someone on the outside to give him perspective. All of us need the same thing. Seek wisdom from the wise, advice from the experienced, and knowledge from the educated. In the process you will become all those things yourself.

Character
Heeding the Right Advice

What Matters Most...

◎ Recognizing the need for advice. Everyone from CEOs to world leaders to everyday folk need advice. Wise people seek advice.

◎ Knowing from whom to get advice. There are many people with opinions, but few with worthwhile advice.

◎ Seeking advice from spiritual people who have insight into God's Word and the Christian faith.

◎ Learning to learn. You grow through teachers and experience.

◎ Knowing that there are absolutes in the world and that God established them. Understanding begins with God.

What Doesn't Matter...

◎ Knowing everything. No one does. There is no shame in asking advice.

◎ Perception. Too many people think asking for advice is a weakness. The reverse is true. Strength is asking for guidance without shame.

◎ Selfish advice. Some advice suggests that causing difficulty for others is right as long as you benefit. It is not.

◎ Contrary advice. Counsel that goes against the proven teaching of the Bible is a stroll down a dangerous path.

◎ Advice that lowers your standards. Morality is still a part of God's plan, and He still takes it seriously.

Focus Points...

Where there is no guidance the people fall, but in abundance of counselors there is victory.
PROVERBS 11:14 NASB

Blessed is the man who does not walk in the counsel of the wicked or stand in the way of sinners or sit in the seat of mockers.
PSALM 1:1 NIV

There are many plans in a man's heart, nevertheless the LORD's counsel—that will stand.
PROVERBS 19:21 NKJV

Teach the wise, and they will be wiser. Teach the righteous, and they will learn more. Fear of the LORD is the beginning of wisdom. Knowledge of the Holy One results in understanding.
PROVERBS 9:9–10 NLT

what really counts

Ointment and perfume rejoice the heart: so doth the sweetness of a man's friend by hearty counsel.
PROVERBS 27:9 KJV

No gift is more precious than good advice.

ERASMUS

Do not open your heart to every man, but discuss your affairs with one who is wise and who fears God.

THOMAS À KEMPIS

Character
Wall to Wall

He that hath no rule over his own spirit is like a city that is broken down, and without walls.

PROVERBS 25:28 KJV

what really counts

Walls surrounded ancient cities. If the city was important, it had a wall and for good reason. Walls kept out what should stay out (animals, invaders, thieves) and kept in what belonged in (citizens, supplies, leaders). Some of these walls were enormous. Nineveh's walls were wide enough for three chariots to ride side by side along the top. Babylon had walls eighty-seven feet wide. The entire Old Testament book of Nehemiah is about the rebuilding of Jerusalem's walls. A city whose walls were broken down or in need of repair was considered a disgrace.

Such walls became a euphemism for self-control. That was King Solomon's point in the proverb above. Self-control is a strength; lack of such control is a weakness. Taking responsibility for our words, thoughts, and actions keeps us spiritually, mentally, and emotionally strong and protected. When we fail to shore up our spiritual defenses, we run the risk of failure.

William Mulholland achieved many engineering feats, but he will always be remembered for the failure of the Saint Francis Dam in San Francisquito Canyon, California. A few minutes before midnight on March 12, 1928, the dam gave way and some five hundred people lost their lives. Water that reached a height of eighty feet destroyed everything in its path. The bitterly sad part of the story was that the dam had begun leaking the day before and Mulholland and others knew it, but they didn't think it mattered. Mulholland meant no harm. The Department of Water and Power valued life as much as anyone. They just didn't believe that the leaks they were seeing could result in the damage that occurred.

That's the challenge for us—to be aware of our spiritual walls. Are they keeping out what belongs out, and are they keeping in what belongs in? Self-control is a sign of sturdy walls; lack of it indicates trouble. God has given control of our spirits to us. It's a wonderful privilege, but one that must be taken seriously. The story of the Trojan horse is well-known. Greek soldiers built a hollow horse to hide in and left it like a gift for the citizens of Troy. The horse was pulled in, and while the city slept, the Greek soldiers exited the horse and laid waste to the city. The Trojans let in their own destruction. We are responsible for what enters our minds and our hearts. We build and maintain the walls. What condition are your walls in?

Character
Wall to Wall

What Matters Most...

◎ Understanding that you have walls and for good reason. There are things to keep out and things to keep in.

◎ Knowing that walls require care and attention. If you don't care for them, no one else will.

◎ Your mental and spiritual walls make up your self-control. If you have no self-control, you have no protective walls.

◎ Strong walls are set on a strong foundation, which is a solid relationship with Christ.

◎ Every wall has a gate, and you are the gatekeeper. Self-control thinks about whom or what it lets in.

What Doesn't Matter...

◎ What others are doing. You are responsible for your actions and choices. Avoid mimicking the bad choices of others.

◎ The mistakes of your past don't matter. The choices you make today do. It's never too late to start making good decisions.

◎ Greed. Greed is an appetite without control; it is desire without thought. It lives for the moment.

◎ Temptation. He who controls the gate owns the city. Temptation wants the keys, but obedience is better than temptation—every time.

Focus Points...

Everyone who competes in the games exercises self-control in all things. They then do it to receive a perishable wreath, but we an imperishable.
1 CORINTHIANS 9:25 NASB

There is a way that seems right to a man, but its end is the way of death.
PROVERBS 16:25 NKJV

Make every effort to add to your faith goodness; and to goodness, knowledge; and to knowledge, self-control; and to self-control, perseverance; and to perseverance, godliness; and to godliness, brotherly kindness; and to brotherly kindness, love.
2 PETER 1:5–7 NIV

When the Holy Spirit controls our lives, he will produce this kind of fruit in us: love, joy, peace, patience, kindness, goodness, faithfulness, gentleness, and self-control. Here there is no conflict with the law.
GALATIANS 5:22–23 NLT

what really counts

Self-control is the mother of spiritual health.
SAINT JOHN CLIMACUS

He who reigns within himself, and rules passions, desires, and fears, is more than a king.
JOHN MILTON

Character
Speech Therapy

A gentle answer turns away wrath, but a harsh word stirs up anger. The tongue of the wise makes knowledge acceptable, but the mouth of fools spouts folly.

PROVERBS 15:1–2 NASB

what really counts

There isn't a single aspect of our lives that isn't touched by words. Words are spoken, written, and broadcast thoughts. Words travel short distances, sometimes just across the dining room table, or they can travel great distances. "Houston, the Eagle has landed." Neil Armstrong spoke those words from the moon's surface a quarter million miles away from earth. Words carry great impact. Think of the emotions involved with "President Kennedy has been shot" or "Will you marry me?" Despite this, words are the most underrated items in our world. We know this because we use words so carelessly, without giving thought to their effect.

The Bible provides us with a little "speech therapy." It's something we all need. Words spoken without thought not only hurt those around us; they can also hurt us. In December 1825 there was an unsuccessful attempt to topple the Russian czar Nicholas I. Kondraty Ryleyev participated in that revolt and was condemned to be hanged. He was, but the rope broke and he toppled to the ground. He struggled to his feet and once the noose was removed from around his neck, he said, "In Russia they do not know how to do anything properly, not even how to make a rope." Hearing of this, Czar Nicholas said, "Well, let the contrary be proved."

We can use words to lie or to build up; to injure or to comfort; to disappoint or to inspire. The choice remains ours. Words are free to use, but they carry a cost. The Bible teaches that we are responsible for our words and comments. When we learn to control our speech, we learn to control our lives. Careless words are proof of a careless mind and a reckless heart. Words spoken for the benefit of others are proof of wisdom and mental depth.

The New Testament writer James gave some of the greatest advice ever given. He said that people should be quick to hear and slow to speak. Our culture has turned that around. Too often we are quick to speak and slow to hear . . . or think. The old country philosopher said, "There was a reason God gave us two ears and only one mouth." Every day is a new opportunity to control our speech, put away swearing and curses, and instead speak words that matter, words that make a difference in life.

Character
Speech Therapy

What Matters Most...

◎ Knowing that words, like dynamite, can be used for good or bad.

◎ Knowing that disciplined speech is proof of a disciplined mind and heart.

◎ Understanding that the effects of what takes a few seconds to say may last a lifetime.

◎ Realizing that one of the few truly impossible things in the world is the ability to take back something said.

◎ Believing that your words say more about you than your dress, income, home, or success.

What Doesn't Matter...

◎ Silence. There is nothing to fear in silence, and words need not be spoken to fill the void.

◎ Volume. Loud words do not make you right; they just make you noisy.

◎ Being believed. No one can persuade the one who refuses to be convinced. If one's ears aren't open, talking will not unplug them.

◎ The last word. There's no such thing. The conversation may end, but thoughts continue on.

◎ Vocabulary. Vocabulary is a powerful tool, but a kind heart and a soft word are far more convincing.

Focus Points...

This you know, my beloved brethren. But everyone must be quick to hear, slow to speak and slow to anger; for the anger of man does not achieve the righteousness of God.
JAMES 1:19–20 NASB

Speaking the truth in love, we will in all things grow up into him who is the Head, that is, Christ.
EPHESIANS 4:15 NIV

Let your speech always be with grace, seasoned with salt, that you may know how you ought to answer each one.
COLOSSIANS 4:6 NKJV

Don't talk too much, for it fosters sin. Be sensible and turn off the flow!
PROVERBS 10:19 NLT

what really counts

Deliver my soul, O LORD, from lying lips, from a deceitful tongue.
PSALM 120:2 NASB

Words which do not give the light of Christ increase the darkness.

MOTHER TERESA

Not only to say the right thing in the right place, but far more difficult, to leave unsaid the wrong thing at the tempting moment.

GEORGE SALA

Character
Saints: The Privilege of Calling

> O fear the LORD, you His saints;
> for to those who fear Him there
> is no want.
>
> PSALM 34:9 NASB

what really counts

"I'm no saint." You've probably heard someone say that. Perhaps you've said it yourself. The truth is there are far more saints than most people realize. To most, a saint is someone who is perfect in all they do. Either they are not plagued by the temptations and failures we experience or they have somehow overcome such problems to live a life so amazing that no one can measure up to the reputation. That is not a saint. At least, it's not the biblical definition of the term. In the Old Testament, the Hebrew word translated as *saint* refers to something "set apart for God." The word is used 116 times. The New Testament word means the same thing, except it refers to people rather than objects.

A saint is someone who has a relationship to God through Jesus Christ. Their sainthood is not based on miracles they performed, powerful sermons they preached, or missionary journeys they took. Saints are just ordinary people of faith. They might be schoolteachers, mechanics, doctors, laborers, designers, writers, or plumbers. Instead of a halo, they might wear a baseball cap.

Saints are chosen people. They are "called" people, and it is God who does the calling. Believers are saints not because they've reached perfection but because their faith has set them apart for God. Saints see the world through the eyes of faith. They know that there is more to this life than can be seen. Their faith has separated them from their old way of living to a life lived for God. No one does that perfectly. It is the heartfelt effort that counts.

When we believe, God sets us apart. We are changed within. We live our lives like millions have before us. We have families, we run businesses, we face problems, we laugh. In short, life continues on, but it does so with a spiritual perspective and an unbreakable connection to God. Every day, we look at a piece of glass that has been silvered on the back. We call it a mirror, and it reflects our image back to us. You as a person of faith can look in that mirror and see a saint—set apart by God, for God. Your faith makes you a saint, even if you can't see a halo.

Character
Saints: The Privilege of Calling

What Matters Most...

- ◎ Faith, the connecting belief that changes what was to what is and what can be.

- ◎ Understanding that God cares enough to call you and set you apart for an unbreakable relationship with Him.

- ◎ The way you walk through life, living like a person of belief and daily faith.

- ◎ Seeing yourself as a saint who lives each day for the God who loves you.

- ◎ Being forgiven. Saints are not perfect people, just forgiven people.

What Doesn't Matter...

- ◎ Halos. Saints look like everyone else, but they are different on the inside.

- ◎ Perfection. Saints and sinners look alike for a reason. The difference is that saints care about their sin.

- ◎ A seminary degree. Believers should learn as much as they can about their faith, but complete knowledge isn't a prerequisite. Faith is.

- ◎ Being ordinary. There have been great and inspirational saints in the past. Your life can inspire someone else.

- ◎ Yesterday. Today's choices are more important.

Focus Points...

He gave some as apostles, and some as prophets, and some as evangelists, and some as pastors and teachers, for the equipping of the saints for the work of service, to the building up of the body of Christ.

EPHESIANS 4:11–12 NASB

Dear friends, although I was very eager to write to you about the salvation we share, I felt I had to write and urge you to contend for the faith that was once for all entrusted to the saints.

JUDE 1:3 NIV

To all who are in Rome, beloved of God, called to be saints: Grace to you and peace from God our Father and the Lord Jesus Christ.

ROMANS 1:7 NKJV

what really counts

We are writing to the church of God in Corinth, you who have been called by God to be his own holy people. He made you holy by means of Christ Jesus, just as he did all Christians everywhere—whoever calls upon the name of Jesus Christ, our Lord and theirs.

1 CORINTHIANS 1:2 NLT

What is the Church if not the assembly of all the saints?

SAINT IGNATIUS

A man does not have to be an angel in order to be a saint.

ALBERT SCHWEITZER

213

Character

Stewards: The Privilege of Management

> Let a man so consider us, as servants of Christ and stewards of the mysteries of God. Moreover it is required in stewards that one be found faithful.
>
> 1 Corinthians 4:1–2 NKJV

what really counts

There are many images of God. Some people see Him as an elderly man with a long white beard. Other people portray Him as a king who sits upon a heavenly throne. Imagine if God were the CEO and chairman of the board of a large corporation. Maybe it's called Universe Incorporated. Perhaps there would be a tagline: "Involving the created with the Creator." The mission statement might be: "To bridge the gap between the Divine and the mortal and to bring eternal life to all who believe."

Who would sit around the boardroom table? All three persons of the Godhead—Father, Son, and Holy Spirit—would be there, of course, but who else? The apostle Peter? No, he's retired. If there were such a divine boardroom table, you would be one of the people seated around its perimeter. Sound strange? It does to those people who don't see the important roles they play in God's plan. Every believer is on

God's management team; every Christian is an executive with an assigned responsibility. The biblical term for such a person is *steward*.

A steward is someone who has been given the responsibility to care for another person's property, money, and possessions. God has assigned to His followers the task of making the most of their gifts, possessions, money, relationships, and everything else He has given to them. It is hard to imagine an infinite God trusting finite people with the business of His kingdom, but God has done exactly that. Everything we have, everything we own, and every skill we possess has been given for a reason, and as executives in the kingdom of God, it is our duty to use God's investment in us.

Not only is God involved in our business, but we are also involved in His. That is the principle of stewardship—using what God has given us to His glory. This requires a new mind-set for many. It necessitates that we look at everything we do and own in light of management. *Management* is another good term for *stewardship*. We are managers who have been given various skills and resources to serve God. In a sense, our faith has given us a promotion. God has said, "Take what I have given you, and do something with it." He has trusted us to manage our lives, our families, our health, our money, and our possessions. It feels good to be trusted so much.

Character
Stewards: The Privilege of Management

What Matters Most...

◎ Recognizing the privilege of being on God's management team.

◎ Changing your perspective to see your possessions as investments from God.

◎ A godly view of material wealth. Money is not evil, but the love of money is.

◎ Using what you have to the benefit of God's kingdom and the help of His people.

◎ ROI—Return On Investment. What you have has not been given for you to sit on, but to use.

What Doesn't Matter...

◎ Amount. Some people have been given more, and consequently they bear more responsibility. How much you have been given is secondary to what you do with it.

◎ History. Very often you come to see your responsibility later in life. It's never too late to get started on stewardship.

◎ Failure. It is more important to have faithfully tried and failed than to never have tried at all.

◎ What other people have. Stewardship is not a competition with others or even with yourself; it is doing the best you can with what you've been given.

Focus Points...

If the master returns and finds that the servant has done a good job, there will be a reward. I assure you, the master will put that servant in charge of all he owns.
MATTHEW 24:46–47 NLT

Whoever can be trusted with very little can also be trusted with much, and whoever is dishonest with very little will also be dishonest with much.
LUKE 16:10 NIV

God is not unjust to forget your work and labor of love which you have shown toward His name, in that you have ministered to the saints, and do minister.
HEBREWS 6:10 NKJV

Don't forget to do good and to share what you have with those in need, for such sacrifices are very pleasing to God.
HEBREWS 13:16 NLT

what really counts

All the blessings we enjoy are Divine deposits, committed to our trust on this condition, that they should be dispensed for the benefit of our neighbors.
JOHN CALVIN

We deem it a sacred responsibility and a genuine opportunity to be faithful stewards of all God has entrusted to us: our time, our talents, and our financial resources. We view all of life as a sacred trust to be used wisely.
MORAVIAN COVENANT OF CHRISTIAN LIVING

217

Character
The Most Important Thing You Do

> Though you have not seen him, you love
> him; and even though you do not see him
> now, you believe in him and are filled with
> an inexpressible and glorious joy.
>
> 1 PETER 1:8 NIV

what really counts

In the book of Exodus are some very famous command-ments. We call them the Ten Commandments. Fourteen hundred years after Moses received those words from God, Jesus said, "A new command I give you: Love one another. As I have loved you, so you must love one another" (John 13:34 NIV). The religious leaders of the day counted 613 commandments in the Old Testament. Some they considered "heavy" and others "light" commandments. We need commandments. They provide a structure to our lives like studs form a wall or girders support a bridge.

When asked which of all the commandments was the most important, Jesus said there were two: First, to love God with our entire being; and second, to love our neighbors as ourselves. The first enables the second. In short, loving God is the most important thing we do.

Every school-aged child is familiar with tetherball. The game is played around a tall metal pole to which a ball is attached by a rope—a tether. The players stand opposite each other and hit the ball when it swings to their side. No matter how hard the child strikes the ball, it never goes far. The rope keeps it in play. Our love for God is an unbreakable tether. Once we are attached to God through faith, we are there for keeps. Our love anchors us to the Creator as sure as the rope holds the tetherball in place.

Unlike an inanimate rope, however, our tether is strong and vital. Our love is a connection that flows from us to God and from God to us. In all that we do during the days of our lives, nothing is as important as loving God. From that love spring our motives, our desires, our direction, our hope, our longing, our wisdom, and countless things more. We can and should love God with our hearts, our minds, and our very souls. Saint Augustine came to God after living a very loose life, but when he came, he gave God his all. So in love with God was Saint Augustine that he prayed, "Lord, hast Thou declared that no man shall see Thy face and live?—then let me die, that I may see Thee." The first and last act of his day was to love God. It was the most important thing he did. It is the most important thing we do.

Character
The Most Important Thing You Do

What Matters Most...

- ◎ God is lovable. He is not distant, cold, or aloof. He is there.

- ◎ God desires your love. Your love brings Him joy. Your love is a gift to Him.

- ◎ Loving God makes a difference in the present. Love is never wasted.

- ◎ Loving God changes you from the inside out. You may not have all the answers, but you do know that love given to God is love that is always returned.

- ◎ Loving God helps you understand God's loving you. No one can out-give or out-love God.

What **Doesn't** Matter...

- ◎ Emotion. Emotion is important, but love goes well beyond feeling; it comes from every area of your life.

- ◎ Sight. You do not have to see God to experience His love or to share your love with Him.

- ◎ Logic. It may be odd to realize that the more you love God, the more your capacity to love Him grows. Still, it is true.

- ◎ Sin. Everyone has and does sin. The most powerful force to resisting temptation is to love God more and more.

- ◎ Hectic schedules. You are a busy person, but there is always time to tell God you love Him.

Focus Points...

Jesus answered, "The foremost is, 'Hear, O Israel! the Lord our God is one Lord; and you shall love the Lord your God with all your heart, and with all your soul, and with all your mind, and with all your strength.' The second is this, 'you shall love your neighbor as yourself.' There is no other commandment greater than these."
MARK 12:29–31 NASB

Hear, O Israel: The LORD our God, the LORD is one.
DEUTERONOMY 6:4 NIV

If someone says, "I love God," and hates his brother, he is a liar; for he who does not love his brother whom he has seen, how can he love God whom he has not seen?
1 JOHN 4:20 NKJV

**what
really
counts**

As the hart panteth after the water brooks, so panteth my soul after thee, O God. My soul thirsteth for God, for the living God: when shall I come and appear before God?
PSALM 42:1–2 KJV

Human things must be known to be loved; but divine things must be loved to be known.

BLAISE PASCAL

He who is filled with love is filled with God himself.

SAINT AUGUSTINE OF HIPPO

Character
Choice: The Second Greatest Gift

Our people must learn to devote themselves to doing what is good, in order that they may provide for daily necessities and not live unproductive lives.

TITUS 3:14 NIV

what really counts

Every day we face choices. Even sitting down in a restaurant leads to some decision making: fries or onion rings, blue cheese or ranch, well done or medium rare. Sometimes we face far more important decisions, such as whom to marry, what job to take, which house to buy, which bills to pay. Not long after Christianity began to spread through the world, great persecution broke out. The Roman emperor Trajan instigated one such persecution. One of Trajan's key men was the governor of Bithynia, a man named Pliny. In a letter to the emperor, he told how he distinguished between true Christians and those who just wore the name. He wrote, "I gave these men a chance to invoke the gods of Rome, offer sacrifice to the image of the Emperor, and finally to curse the name of Christ," adding, "none of these acts, those who are really Christians can be forced to do."

It's difficult to imagine those early Christians standing before some magistrate, armed Roman guards nearby, and having to choose between cursing Christ and execution. Yet many people chose to die rather than capitulate to the demands of the persecutors. They made the tough decisions. Often we face tough decisions.

Choice is a power and a gift. Salvation is the greatest gift God has given us. Second to that, however, is the gift of choice. We have been equipped to make life choices. We can choose to believe; we can choose disbelief. Trust, love, hope, happiness, joy, and just about everything else come from the choices we make.

Making the right choices is sometimes difficult. As with the early Christians we may find ourselves facing decisions we don't want to make—decisions that are filled with emotion, even fear. We grow by our choices. The difference between the drug addict and the one who avoids drugs is the choice to say no. Today you will make choices. And tomorrow you will make more. Prayerful, God-centered choices lead to fulfillment. Sometimes they may take us through difficult times, but godly choices are always the right choices. God has set you free to make choices and to benefit from those decisions or to bear the price that bad choices exact. The good news is that God is there to guide us in the decisions we face if we will pray and listen to the leading He places in our hearts.

Character
Choice: The Second Greatest Gift

What Matters Most...

- Knowing who holds the steering wheel—you. The direction of your life is dictated by the choices you make.

- Realizing that choice is a powerful gift given to you by God. Learn to use it wisely.

- Understanding that making right choices can be difficult but that God strengthens those dedicated to choosing wisely.

- Knowing more about God. The more you know Him and His will, the better the choices you make.

- Choosing to value the power of choice in your life.

What Doesn't Matter...

- Fatalism. You are more victor than victim. You set your own course.

- Past decisions. They can't be undone, but new choices can be made to improve both yourself and the situation.

- Control. No one can control everything in his life. Illnesses come, problems arise. What you can control is your response.

- Setbacks. Nothing in life works perfectly. Learn from bad choices.

- Negative influence. There have always been those who criticize, but your decision remains your own.

Focus Points...

If you are unwilling to serve the Lord, then choose today whom you will serve. Would you prefer the gods your ancestors served beyond the Euphrates? Or will it be the gods of the Amorites in whose land you now live? But as for me and my family, we will serve the Lord.
Joshua 24:15 NLT

Elijah came near to all the people and said, "How long will you hesitate between two opinions? If the Lord is God, follow Him; but if Baal, follow him." But the people did not answer him a word.
1 Kings 18:21 NASB

"You do not want to leave too, do you?" Jesus asked the Twelve. Simon Peter answered him, "Lord, to whom shall we go? You have the words of eternal life. We believe and know that you are the Holy One of God."
John 6:67–69 NIV

what really counts

Let us not become conceited, provoking one another, envying one another.
Galatians 5:26 NKJV

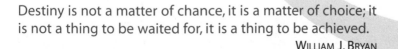

Destiny is not a matter of chance, it is a matter of choice; it is not a thing to be waited for, it is a thing to be achieved.
William J. Bryan

We can try to avoid making choices by doing nothing, but even that is a decision.
Gary Collins

225

Character
Leading Begins with Following

> Sitting down, Jesus called the Twelve and said, "If anyone wants to be first, he must be the very last, and the servant of all."
>
> MARK 9:35 NIV

what really counts

A few decades ago the military was undergoing a transition to "an all-volunteer army." Hearing this, a soldier said to an officer, "Let me know when this becomes a volunteer army. I want to volunteer to be a general." In our society those who lead are held in higher regard than those who follow. Jesus had a different take on the matter. In fact, He taught the opposite. When Jesus began His ministry, He chose twelve men to be His trusted inner circle of disciples. These men would travel wherever He went, hear all His teaching, receive special instruction, and receive unique power. Eleven of them did very well; one—Judas—failed.

Still, the eleven faithful disciples were as human as the rest of us, harboring the same desires and hopes. They, like many of the followers of Christ, believed that Jesus was going to set up an earthly kingdom and run off the occupying Roman army. With that in mind, the mother of two of the

226

disciples approached Jesus, her two adult sons in tow. She got right to the point: "Grant that these two sons of mine may sit, one on Your right hand and the other on the left, in Your kingdom" (Matthew 20:21 NKJV). The request irritated the other ten disciples, and the grumbling began. Jesus had to sit them down and fine-tune their thinking.

Most of us need the same fine-tuning. Now as then, people think that those who direct the work are better than those who do the work. Jesus had a different view. To be a leader, He taught, you must first be a follower. To be first, you must be willing to be last. Leadership stems from servanthood. Jesus practiced what He preached. In the Upper Room in Jerusalem, just hours before Judas would betray Him and with the agonies of the cross just a short time away, Jesus knelt before each of the disciples and washed their feet. An act that not even a Jewish slave could be forced to do, Jesus did willingly.

Leadership isn't marked by one's name on the door of a private office or by one's title, nor is it measured by the size of the paycheck one receives. Leadership is a function of how well one serves others. It is no accident that the conductor who leads the orchestra has his back turned to the crowd. Godly leadership always has the follower in mind.

Character
Leading Begins with Following

What Matters Most...

- ◉ Being not just a leader, but a leader with a purpose.

- ◉ Seeing the value of those who follow you and aiding them in their efforts.

- ◉ Being willing to "wash the feet" of those you lead to show that you esteem their work as highly as you esteem your own.

- ◉ Learning to follow. No one can be a leader who has not first been a follower. Never forget what was learned in those days.

- ◉ The quickest way to the front is to be willing to be last.

What Doesn't Matter...

- ◉ A Title. A title has its place in life, but no title can define a person's heart.

- ◉ Ego. It is a good thing to be proud of achievement, but an overindulgent ego is a sign that your focus has shifted.

- ◉ Glory. The high praise of others is a by-product of what you do, not the goal.

- ◉ Criticism. Every leader is the target of criticism, usually by the envious.

- ◉ An opinion contrary to that of God. God's opinion is what really counts.

Focus Points...

It shall not be so among you: but whosoever will be great among you, let him be your minister; and whosoever will be chief among you, let him be your servant: Even as the Son of man came not to be ministered unto, but to minister, and to give his life a ransom for many.
MATTHEW 20:26–28 KJV

You call me "Teacher" and "Lord," and rightly so, for that is what I am. Now that I, your Lord and Teacher, have washed your feet, you also should wash one another's feet. I have set you an example that you should do as I have done for you. I tell you the truth, no servant is greater than his master, nor is a messenger greater than the one who sent him.
JOHN 13:13–16 NIV

what really counts

Let each of you look out not only for his own interests, but also for the interests of others.
PHILIPPIANS 2:4 NKJV

As each one has received a special gift, employ it in serving one another as good stewards of the manifold grace of God.
1 PETER 4:10 NASB

Leadership is found in becoming the servant of all.
RICHARD FOSTER

The great leader is seen as the servant first.
ROBERT K. GREENLEAF

229

What Matters Most to Me About
Character

Personal growth and character are choices. Outside influences—such as upbringing, opportunities and tragedies, mentors and detractors, and a thousand other things—contribute to the formation of who you are, but the ultimate responsibility rests with you and the decisions you make. The good news is that God is there to help you and guide you and that you have Christ as your example.

◎ *Advice is cheap, and many are those who have gallons of it to give. In your life, whom have you found to be a source of sound advice and reasoned thought? Jot down their names, and then jot down your source of spiritual advice.*

what
really
counts

_____

_____

_____

_____

_____

◎ *Self-control is one of the great challenges you face. Controlling what influences you and what you say is a never-ending struggle. How's your speech? In what condition are your protective walls? Write down two or three areas in which you can improve your speech, and list what outside influences exist that hinder or help.*

_____

_____

_____

_____

_____

People of faith are spiritual executives in God's "corporation" and therefore carry responsibility for the use of their time and energy. Take a few moments to think about all that you have, whether it be much or little, and then ask yourself, "Am I being a good manager of all that God has given me?" Jot down a few thoughts.

_____

_____

_____

_____

_____

_____

_____

_____

_____

Choice is a powerful gift from God. Look back across your life and consider the good and bad choices you made. What did you learn from your mistakes? What did you learn from the right choices? List a few thoughts.

_____

_____

_____

_____

_____

_____

_____

_____

_____

Make a tree good and its fruit will be good, or make a tree bad and its fruit will be bad, for a tree is recognized by its fruit.

MATTHEW 12:33 NIV

PRAYER

An Introduction

> Be anxious for nothing, but in everything by prayer and supplication with thanksgiving let your requests be made known to God.
>
> PHILIPPIANS 4:6 NASB

what really counts

They're everywhere these days. Cell phones hang from hips, sit in purses, and are pressed to ears. Private conversations are made public as people sit in restaurants chatting with someone who may be a few blocks away or across the country. We are a connected people, grafted together by phones, the Internet, and e-mail. We talk by phone, radio, e-mail, and instant messaging. Never before has the world been so in touch with itself. How in touch are we with our Creator?

Prayer is talking to God. It needs no fancy theological definition. Prayer is the simple act of one human communicating with God. It is personal; it can be private. Prayer can take place in a church, in a car, from bed, at a meal; any time, any place. It is easy to do. It may be filled with heartrending anguish, or be bubbling over with joy. Prayer may be sparked by a pressing need or be a heartfelt visit with the Almighty. Children can pray as well as adults.

A. W. Pink said, "Nothing is too great and nothing is too small to commit into the hands of the Lord." The exciting thing about prayer comes when we realize that God is *eager* to hear from us. God never says, "Oh, it's you again."

God has a willing ear, and He leans forward to hear what comes from our lips and from our hearts. Talking to God is an honor and a privilege, and no phone is needed.

> Prayer opens the heart to God, and it is the means by which the soul, though empty, is filled by God.
>
> JOHN BUNYAN

Prayer
Kneeling Tall

When I think of the wisdom and scope of God's plan, I fall to my knees and pray to the Father, the Creator of everything in heaven and on earth.

EPHESIANS 3:14–15 NLT

what really counts

The great American evangelist Dwight L. Moody once stated, "The Christian on his knees sees more than the philosopher on tiptoe." It's an interesting and accurate observation. Moody understood the essence, the power, and the value of prayer. The ancient Jews had three positions of prayer: standing with hands lifted heavenward; kneeling with hands lifted; and facedown with hands turned upward. Which was better? No one position is better than the other. Prayer isn't about body position; it's about heart position. Many people kneel in prayer, and there is merit in that, but what really counts is the prayer itself. Whether we stand, sit, kneel, or fall facedown on the floor, our prayer still shoots heavenward.

It is from the position of prayer that we get our greatest, most piercing view of the world around us, and in us. Prayer puts life into perspective. One cannot spend time talking to

God without being changed in the process. Prayer is to walk into the throne room of God and whisper in His ear. It is also a time when God speaks to hearts and touches souls. Our prayer is God's delight. He is eager to hear from you.

In the early days of the United States, a visitor who knew that George Washington was to be at Congress asked how he could distinguish Washington from the other people present. The answer came, "You can easily distinguish him when Congress goes to prayer. Washington is the gentleman who kneels." Prayer is important for the powerful and the powerless; for the rich and the poor.

When we slip to our knees in prayer, our stature grows; when we close our eyes, our vision improves; when we speak soft words, our thoughts echo in heaven. From a position of prayer—whatever that position might be—we gain a heavenly perspective. The mountaineer sees more from his vantage point than does the villager in the valley. Prayer elevates our souls so that we might see as God sees and see what God would have us see. For the person of faith, prayer is not an additive; it is the heart of spiritual life. While astronomers wonder if there is "intelligent life out there," people of faith know there is and talk to Him every day. Prayer is not limited to the pious or the seemingly perfect; it is open to anyone who is willing to bow his head and begin, "Dear Father in heaven . . ."

Prayer
Kneeling Tall

What Matters Most...

◎ Starting. Today is a good day to speak to God. Now is the time to start.

◎ Continuing. Prayer is a lifestyle. It is more steering wheel than spare tire.

◎ Valuing. Make time for the important and the valuable. Prayer is the most important thing you will do today.

◎ Connecting. Remember that it is God to whom you speak. Be respectful and open.

◎ Believing. Prayer is an act of trust, knowing that God wants to hear from you.

What Doesn't Matter...

◎ Formulas. The basics of prayer can be taught, but the real learning comes from open, honest, simple prayer.

◎ Fancy words. Prayer is a conversation between the created and the Creator. God is not impressed with long, involved prayers. He is impressed when His children visit Him.

◎ Missed opportunities. An active prayer life can begin now.

◎ Being heard by others. In prayer the only listener that counts is God.

◎ Age. God listens to the child and the senior—He is an equal-opportunity listener.

Focus Points...

My heart has heard you say, "Come and talk with me." And my heart responds, "LORD, I am coming."
PSALM 27:8 NLT

When you pray, go into your room, close the door and pray to your Father, who is unseen. Then your Father, who sees what is done in secret, will reward you.
MATTHEW 6:6 NIV

My voice You shall hear in the morning, O LORD; in the morning I will direct it to You, and I will look up.
PSALM 5:3 NKJV

O LORD, You have heard the desire of the humble; You will strengthen their heart, You will incline Your ear.
PSALM 10:17 NASB

When he had taken the book, the four beasts and four and twenty elders fell down before the Lamb, having every one of them harps, and golden vials full of odours, which are the prayers of saints.
REVELATION 5:8 KJV

To pray is to cast off your burdens, it is to tear away your rags, it is to shake off your diseases, it is to be filled with spiritual vigor, it is to reach the highest point of Christian health.

C. H. SPURGEON

Prayer is love in need appealing to love in power.
ROBERT MOFFATT

what really counts

Prayer
The Mouth That Speaks

You will call upon me and come and pray to me, and I will listen to you. You will seek me and find me when you seek me with all your heart.

JEREMIAH 29:12–13 NIV

"Our Father who art in heaven," begins the model prayer. When Jesus uttered these words, He did so because the disciples had asked how to pray. So familiar are these words that we often overlook how powerfully personal they are. Jesus taught us to approach God as our Father. *Father* is an important word. Charles Stanford wrote, "You never say Father, to a force; Father, to a law; Father, to a mist; Father, to a mile, nor to infinite millions of miles in a line; 'Father' is not the name for Thought apart from the Thinker, nor for Friendship apart from the Friend; nor for a Link, though it is the first link in a long chain of a grand phenomena. If we mean more than a figurative father, we mean by that word a living Person."

When we open our mouths to pray, we are not speaking to an impersonal force, or a great something out there. We are speaking to our heavenly Father. This is not a title we humans have chosen for God; it is the title He has chosen for Himself.

Of all the possible titles available—King, Creator, Mighty God, and a thousand more—God chose the personal, sensitive, relational "Father." If called to the White House to meet the president of the United States, protocol would dictate that we stand when he enters and that we refer to him as "Mr. President." If we were to stand before a king, we would address him as "Your Majesty." When we come before God, all pretenses are set aside, and we call Him "Father."

Knowing that makes prayer easier. When we pray we do so as a member of the family, and the One to whom we pray sees Himself the way we should see Him, as an eager parent clinging to the words of His children. We should never be flippant with God, but we can pray to Him openly and honestly, as a child would talk to a kind and loving parent. Knowing this removes the barriers to prayer. What is there to say that God has not heard? What need can you make known that He hasn't seen? What sin could you have committed that He doesn't already know about?

Prayer is an open line to God, who wants to hear the words from our mouths, the cries of our hearts, and the yearnings of our souls.

Prayer
The Mouth That Speaks

What Matters Most...

- The proper view of God, not as an all-powerful ogre, but as the perfect Father.

- An honest approach to God. You can fool people, but you can't fool God, nor is there any need to try.

- Understanding that God already knows your needs and desires. Prayer isn't a means of informing God.

- God hungers for your communication. He doesn't need your information; He desires your presence.

- Prayer is an open line to God.

What **Doesn't** Matter...

- Any previous misconception. False and fearful ideas can be dismissed and proper ones accepted.

- The difference between God and you. You can scarcely conceive of the greatness of God, and your own frailties are too well known. But God still wants to hear from you.

- Not knowing what to say. You communicate with words, but God understands the heart.

- Fear. Everyone has things to be ashamed of, but through prayer that shame can be washed away.

- Time. Short prayers, long prayers, wordless prayers, and structured prayers are all prayer. The key is to simply talk to God.

Focus Points...

Before they call I will answer; while they are still speaking I will hear.
ISAIAH 65:24 NIV

Pray, then, in this way: "Our Father who is in heaven, hallowed be Your name."
MATTHEW 6:9 NASB

Let us therefore come boldly unto the throne of grace, that we may obtain mercy, and find grace to help in time of need.
HEBREWS 4:16 KJV

Always be joyful. Keep on praying. No matter what happens, always be thankful, for this is God's will for you who belong to Christ Jesus.
1 THESSALONIANS 5:16–18 NLT

Hear a just cause, O LORD, attend to my cry; give ear to my prayer which is not from deceitful lips.
PSALM 17:1 NKJV

what really counts

Prayer is the raising of one's mind and heart to God or the requesting of good things from God.
SAINT JOHN DAMASCUS

Prayer is the burden of a sigh, the falling of a tear, the upward glancing of an eye when none but God is near.
JAMES MONTGOMERY

Prayer
The Ear That Hears

> Seek the LORD while he may be
> found; call on him while he is near.
> ISAIAH 55:6 NIV

The president of a large Baptist denomination stood before a gathering of reporters taking questions. After several questions about his background, what he hoped to achieve, and where he thought the denomination was going, one reporter piped up and asked, "Do you talk to God?" The man admitted to praying frequently. "I speak to God all the time." The reporter smiled. "Does He speak to you in an audible voice?" The other reporters snickered. The president smiled and replied, "Oh no. He speaks a whole lot louder than that."

God has spoken audibly to people, but those occasions are rare. Most of the time, God speaks with a different but just as real voice, a voice that touches mind and heart. The key is learning to listen. In the past, military intelligence officers who listened to foreign military broadcasts had to learn to pick out voices buried in meaningless chatter or noise. Part of their training included sitting with headphones pressed to their ears and listening to faint voices speaking in Chinese. This was made difficult because the instructors included squeals and static in the transmissions to the students. They were trying to teach them to focus on the one voice and tune out all the distractions.

God speaks to the heart, but there are many distractions that can draw our attention away. We can learn to listen to the message and not the static. Prayer requires that we speak to God, but it also requires that we listen for His direction. No one likes to be on the receiving end of a one-sided conversation.

The apostle Paul encouraged the early Christians to pray "without ceasing." By that he meant that we should live in an attitude of prayer, our thoughts frequently flying to God. With that comes the idea that we should listen without ceasing. Some of the strongest communication comes without words. Words can be misunderstood; terms ill-defined; intent lost. God speaks to our hearts, granting us peace about decisions or unsettling us when we start down the wrong path. As we learn to pray, so we learn to listen to the small but undeniable voice of God. Coupled with the teaching of the Bible, we can face each day as it comes with wisdom and confidence. In the moments and minutes of prayer, let your voice be heard, your needs known, your longings described—but then listen patiently for the direction of God.

Prayer
The Ear That Hears

What Matters Most...

◎ Pausing in prayerful conversation to gain a sense of what God wants you to do.

◎ Learning to listen with more than your ears; to listen with the heart.

◎ Knowing that God may never speak to you in an audible voice. He may speak in a much louder way.

◎ Maintaining a constant, ceaseless attitude of prayer while remaining open to the leadership of God.

◎ Giving God time to respond to your prayers.

What Doesn't Matter...

◎ Hearing a voice. God seldom speaks to the ear; He speaks to the mind, heart, and soul.

◎ Rote prayers. Reciting the same thing over and over isn't prayer. Prayer is conversation between two people.

◎ Having the right words. Some things are shared with God through heartfelt emotion; some things are shared through groanings that lack terms. God speaks the language of your heart.

◎ A busy schedule. No schedule is so full that there isn't time for prayer. Prayer is a choice.

◎ The length of prayer. Prayer can last moments or hours. It isn't a function of time; rather, it is a function of the heart and godly focus.

Focus Points...

LORD, You have heard the desire of the humble; You will prepare their heart; You will cause Your ear to hear.
PSALM 10:17 NKJV

In the same way the Spirit also helps our weakness; for we do not know how to pray as we should, but the Spirit Himself intercedes for us with groanings too deep for words; and He who searches the hearts knows what the mind of the Spirit is, because He intercedes for the saints according to the will of God.
ROMANS 8:26–27 NASB

This is the confidence that we have in him, that, if we ask any thing according to his will, he heareth us: And if we know that he hear us, whatsoever we ask, we know that we have the petitions that we desired of him.
1 JOHN 5:14–15 KJV

what really counts

Devote yourselves to prayer with an alert mind and a thankful heart.
COLOSSIANS 4:2 NLT

If God does not give us what we crave, He will give us what we need.

THOMAS WATSON

I used to ask God to help me. Then I asked if I might help Him. I ended up by asking Him to do His work through me.
JAMES HUDSON TAYLOR

What Matters Most to Me About
Prayer

Prayer is the most underrated power in the world. The basic notion that God is willing to hear from His people is soul shaking. Not only is He willing to listen, but He also longs to listen. The sound of your voice is precious to Him.

◎ *Prayer life takes practice. It requires that you think of God frequently and be willing to converse with Him about any and every matter, small or large. Write down something you can praise God for, something you need help with, and someone you can pray for.*

_____

_____

_____

_____

_____

_____

_____

◎ *God seldom whispers in your ear. He usually speaks in your heart. This is a new type of listening. Open yourself to the moving of God in your heart. Write down what you think He may be leading you to do.*

_____

_____

_____

_____

_____

_____

what really counts

Honesty is important in prayer. That means sharing your hurts, concerns, and even anger with God. Remember, He already knows what you think and feel, so be open. But prayer also requires that you be willing to hear what God has to say. Finish the sentence "I want to speak to God about . . ."

_____

_____

_____

_____

_____

_____

_____

Prayer goes beyond words. Sometimes you may not know what to ask for, what direction to seek, or what words to use. God listens to the words of your heart as well as the words of your mouth. Jot down areas of confusion that you want to ask God about. If you don't have the words, then just list the concepts (hurt, sadness, fear, hope, desire). God knows what you mean.

_____

_____

_____

_____

_____

_____

_____

_____

When you pray, go into your room, close the door and pray to your Father, who is unseen. Then your Father, who sees what is done in secret, will reward you.

MATTHEW 6:6 NIV

Sin

An Introduction

> If we confess our sins, he is faithful and just to forgive us our sins, and to cleanse us from all unrighteousness.
>
> 1 JOHN 1:9 KJV

what really counts

Jussi Salonoja makes sausage for a living. In Finland he is known as the "Sausage King." His business has made him a wealthy man. Mr. Salonoja also likes to drive fast. On February 11, 2004, he was stopped by Helsinki police for speeding. He had been driving 80 kph (kilometers per hour) in a 40 kph zone—twice the posted speed limit.

This was not new for the young businessman. Four years before, he had been stopped and fined for driving at 200 kph on the highway. He paid a substantial fine. This time, the fine was worse. In Finland, fines are based on income. Since Mr. Salonoja is a millionaire, he was fined the equivalent of $217,000 in U.S. money.

His sins found him out, and there was a price to pay. Imagine that you have a fine like that but you lack the money to pay. Now imagine that someone from the back of the court steps forward and offers to pay the fine. It would be an amazing act of love. Christ did that and more when He paid the price for our sins.

Sin is a heavy burden to bear, and the weight of it can squeeze all the joy out of life. Sin stands between us and God like a gigantic wall. But Jesus took care of all that. Everyone sins. That is one thing every human has in common. The solution to sin is available to all who ask. The key is in the asking.

Sin is essentially a departure from God.

MARTIN LUTHER

Sin
Last Minute

> He said, "Jesus, remember me when you come into your kingdom." Jesus answered him, "I tell you the truth, today you will be with me in paradise."
>
> LUKE 23:42–43 NIV

what really counts

One of the most poignant accounts in the Bible comes from those dark hours when Christ was hanging on the cross. He was a sinless man dying on a cross constructed for another person. To both sides of Him were men who had been arrested and found guilty for their evil deeds. Like Jesus, they were just a short distance from death. At first both mocked Jesus, but something happened to one of them. He understood that he was dying for deeds he had done, but Jesus was dying for what others had done. Hanging above the ground, nails driven through hands and feet, this unnamed man turned to Jesus and asked to be remembered. "Today," Jesus replied through the pain, "you will be with Me in paradise."

It is ironic: A guilty man in the last moments of life asked forgiveness of an innocent man who shared his fate. And Jesus took time out from dying to promise paradise. Here was a man with no biography, no religious experience, no future, reaching out to Jesus at the last minute and finding that Jesus was available. At the most unlikely of places, the most unlikely of men made an unlikely request and received a very Jesus response. In the midst of dying for the world, Jesus took time to take in one more believer—a believer who arrived at faith at the last possible moment.

This short dialogue between sinner and Savior reveals the very heart of Christ. "The Son of Man came to seek and to save what was lost," Jesus said (Luke 19:10 NIV). That was His goal in the beginning, and it continues to be the goal today. One wonders what this man's life might have been like had he come to Jesus earlier. We'll never know, but the important thing is that he came to Christ, even if it was at the very last moment.

Waiting until the last moment to ask Christ into our lives is unwise, but it's wonderful to know that Jesus never gives up on us. There is always room for one more. Whether the decision to follow Christ comes when one is a child or when one is on his deathbed, the door is always open, and on the other side of that door is a very happy Jesus. Sooner is better. Jesus offers a life of meaning, joy, strength, and much more. Why wait until the last minute?

Sin
Last Minute

What Matters Most...

◎ A decision to ask Jesus to be your Lord and Savior. There is no more important decision.

◎ The opportunity of today. This moment is the best moment to receive Jesus.

◎ Knowing that Jesus accepts you at any stage of life. As long as there is life, there is opportunity.

◎ Realizing how great a love Christ has for you. His arms are always open.

What Doesn't Matter...

◎ Your former life. Jesus accepted the dying thief; He'll accept you too, regardless of your history.

◎ Regret. Regret might be a fine motivator, but it changes nothing. Christ changes everything.

◎ Timing. Perhaps too many years have passed, but in the light of eternity those years don't amount to much. The future begins now.

◎ The opinions of others. There were two thieves on crosses that day. Only one turned to Jesus. The other died as he had lived.

◎ Reputation. It doesn't matter how others see you. What matters is what Christ sees and what He can make of you.

Focus Points...

The Son of Man came to seek and to save what was lost.
LUKE 19:10 NIV

God did not send His Son into the world to condemn the world, but that the world through Him might be saved.
JOHN 3:17 NKJV

[John] saw Jesus coming to him and said, "Behold, the Lamb of God who takes away the sin of the world!"
JOHN 1:29 NASB

This is the will of him that sent me, that every one which seeth the Son, and believeth on him, may have everlasting life: and I will raise him up at the last day.
JOHN 6:40 KJV

what really counts

He is the sacrifice for our sins. He takes away not only our sins but the sins of all the world.
1 JOHN 2:2 NLT

Years of repentance are necessary in order to blot out a sin in the eyes of men, but one tear of repentance suffices with God.

FRENCH PROVERB

Jesus accepts you the way you are, but loves you too much to leave you that way.

LEE VENDEN

253

Sin
Forgiveness in God's Plan

I will set out and go back to my father and say to him: Father, I have sinned against heaven and against you.

LUKE 15:18 NIV

what really counts

Noel Coward, as a joke, sent the following message to some of the most influential people in his city: "I know what you did, and if I were you, I'd leave town." They did. Those men were harboring the guilt of having done deeds that embarrassed them, and when they thought they had been discovered, they fled. That's the way it is with sin. It burrows deep in our guts, and we fear that it will come out someday. There are very few people, if any, who need to be convinced that they are sinners. We all sin. Some own up to it; others try to hide the fact in the dark recesses of their minds. When it comes to sin, we're all in the same boat.

There's good news in all of this: God's heart's desire is to forgive us. Too many people see God as eager to strike each sinner with a life-ending bolt of lightning, but the reverse is true. God longs to forgive sin. That's why He sent Jesus. As writer Roy Lessin wrote, "If our greatest need had been infor-

254

mation, God would have sent us an educator; if our greatest need had been technology, God would have sent us a scientist; if our greatest need had been money, God would have sent us an economist; if our greatest need had been pleasure, God would have sent us an entertainer; but our greatest need was forgiveness, so God sent us a Savior."

Forgiveness comes with the asking. Asking comes from acknowledging the need. How do we ask for forgiveness? No magic formula. No incantation. No special words beyond "I'm sorry. Please forgive me." All we need is a heart-to-heart talk with God.

Who receives forgiveness? Those who know they have a need to be forgiven, and all that takes is honesty; those who care about their sin, and all that takes is sensitivity; those who turn to God through Christ, and all that takes is a decision; and those who bother to ask, and all that takes is prayer. God has promised to forgive, and in doing so He meets His desire and our need. It all begins with confession. Confession means to "agree with." When we confess our sins, we are agreeing with God that we need forgiveness. God doesn't need to be informed of our sins—He already knows. We, however, need to know of our forgiveness.

Sin
Forgiveness in God's Plan

What Matters Most...

- Knowing that you are a sinner. No one is exempt. No one is alone.

- Knowing that there is forgiveness of sins—of every sin.

- Understanding that Jesus has done for you what you cannot do for yourself—wipe away your sin.

- Confessing. Confession brings awareness; repentance brings forgiveness.

- Experiencing the relief that forgiveness brings.

What **Doesn't** Matter...

- Guilt. Guilt is a good alarm, but it does not bring the cure.

- Constant regret. God forgives and forgets; so should you.

- Degrees of sin. Sin is sin, and Jesus paid the same price for small and large sins.

- Self-hatred. If God forgives you, then you should forgive yourself.

- The lure of sin. Forgiveness is not an excuse to sin; it is an escape from sin.

Focus Points...

You, being dead in your trespasses and the uncircumcision of your flesh, He has made alive together with Him, having forgiven you all trespasses, having wiped out the handwriting of requirements that was against us, which was contrary to us. And He has taken it out of the way, having nailed it to the cross.
COLOSSIANS 2:13–14 NKJV

God demonstrates His own love toward us, in that while we were yet sinners, Christ died for us.
ROMANS 5:8 NASB

To him give all the prophets witness, that through his name whosoever believeth in him shall receive remission of sins.
ACTS 10:43 KJV

"Come now, let us argue this out," says the LORD. "No matter how deep the stain of your sins, I can remove it. I can make you as clean as freshly fallen snow. Even if you are stained as red as crimson, I can make you as white as wool."
ISAIAH 1:18 NLT

God has cast our confessed sins into the sea, and He's even put a "No Fishing" sign over the spot.

D. L. MOODY

It is always the case that when the Christian looks back, he is looking at the forgiveness of sins.

KARL BARTH

What Matters Most to Me About
Sin

The fact that people are sinners should surprise no one. No rational person says, "I'm sinless." Everyone has sinned and fallen short of the glory of God. The beautiful thing is that God has done something about sin.

⊙ *Sin is missing the mark. Many people wish to skip the whole topic, but while there is no pleasure in sin, there is great joy in forgiveness. The first step is to own up to the problem. Muster up your courage and finish the sentence "I have a sin problem with . . ." If you feel comfortable doing so, write it down; otherwise just make a mental note.*

what
really
counts

⊙ *The solution to sin is not a thing but a person. Jesus bore your sin to the cross so that you could have full and complete pardon. God remembers your sin no more. But sin must be confessed. Take a moment to think of the sins you need to ask forgiveness for.*

Regret is a powerful emotion. You may often regret what you've done, and that regret becomes sadness when you understand that you can't unwind the clock. The thief on the cross took advantage of the moment to turn to Christ and ask to be included. What do you need Jesus to do for you?

_____

_____

_____

_____

_____

_____

_____

_____

Christ received the thief on the cross right then. There was no hesitancy on Jesus' part. That hasn't changed. Write "Jesus, remember me when You come into Your kingdom." Read it out loud.

_____

_____

_____

_____

_____

_____

_____

_____

With the heart one believes unto righteousness, and with the mouth confession is made unto salvation.

ROMANS 10:10 NKJV

SIN

RELATIONSHIPS

An Introduction

> Jesus replied: " 'Love the Lord your God with all your heart and with all your soul and with all your mind.' This is the first and greatest commandment. And the second is like it: 'Love your neighbor as yourself.' All the Law and the Prophets hang on these two commandments."
>
> MATTHEW 22:37–40 NIV

what really counts

A teacher tested her students with a question about the present Seven Wonders of the World. She expected to hear a list like: (1) the Great Pyramid, (2) the Taj Majal, (3) the Grand Canyon, (4) the Panama Canal, (5) the Empire State building, (6) Saint Peter's Basilica, and (7) the Great Wall of China. One girl seemed to be having trouble with the question but finally turned her paper in. Her answers were unexpected. "The Seven Wonders of the World are: to see, to hear, to touch, to taste, to feel, to laugh, and to love."

Of all the things we humans build, nothing is more important or impressive than relationships. Perhaps that is why maintaining relationships can be difficult.

We are imperfect people trying to love other imperfect people. No matter how difficult the task, it is worth the effort.

"Use your head to handle yourself; use your heart to handle others." It's a great piece of advice. In any relationship, whether family, friend, or fellow worker, we need to be able to use heart and mind. We have the privilege of investing ourselves in those around us as others have invested in us.

Mind and heart are the two sides of the same balance. All mind, and we miss out on love, friendship, joy, and the like. All heart, and we have very little wisdom to share and learn nothing from our relationships. Together, mind and heart work miracles around us.

You can never establish a personal relationship without opening up your own heart.

PAUL TOURNIER

Relationships
A Smooth Heart

Every day they continued to meet together in the temple courts. They broke bread in their homes and ate together with glad and sincere hearts, praising God and enjoying the favor of all the people. And the Lord added to their number daily those who were being saved.

ACTS 2:46–47 NIV

what really counts

The human heart is an amazing thing. It beats an average of 75 times a minute, 40 million times a year, or 2.8 billion times during a life of 75 years. With every beat, the adult heart pumps about four ounces of blood. This amounts to 3,000 gallons a day, or 650,000 gallons a year. But the heart is more than a cardiac muscle. To the doctor it might seem a four-chambered pump, but to most of us it is much more. Think of the terms we use: black-hearted, brokenhearted, heartsick, hardhearted, near and dear to the heart, heartthrob, heart and soul, heart smart, heart to heart, heartache, heartbreak; a person can be heartened or heartfelt; we can work heartily and with heartiness; we speak of certain places as being in the heartland; we speak of heartrending, heartstrings, and heart-warming. But most have never heard of a "smooth heart."

In the New Testament book of Acts it is written that the early Christians "ate together with glad and sincere hearts." The word translated *sincere hearts* is literally "smooth hearts." The original term means "without stones." The image is of a farmer's field free of rocks and ready to be plowed. A smooth heart is a heart that is free of the stones of bitterness, resentment, jealousy, envy, and other negative emotions. Spiritual matters require that we have a smooth, uncluttered heart.

Centuries ago, a man wrote a Christian tract called "Come to Jesus." It was widely read and had a powerful influence on the lives of thousands. Years later, he was embroiled in a dispute over some theological principle, so he wrote another tract. The new publication was filled with harsh words, accusations, and vicious comments. He showed the tract to a friend and asked, "What should I title this?" His friend read it and then replied, "Call it 'Go to the Devil,' by the author of 'Come to Jesus.'" The point was made, and the author destroyed the tract.

As we deal with family, friends, neighbors, and workmates, we should do so with a smooth heart—a heart filled with the strength of love and truth. It begins with recognition of the attitudes that need to go and ends with a commitment to treat others as we want to be treated.

Relationships
A Smooth Heart

What Matters Most...

◉ Knowing that you choose your attitudes. The responsibility rests with you.

◉ You have the opportunity to choose a "smooth" heart—a sincere, simple, generous, humble, joyful heart.

◉ Realizing that anyone can be cruel, but with determination you can treat others the way you yourself wish to be treated.

◉ Remembering that you tend to be treated the way you treat others.

◉ Understanding that "stone removal" is an ongoing job. It takes determination and vigilance.

What **Doesn't** Matter...

◉ The choices of others. You are responsible for your actions, not theirs.

◉ Your natural tendencies. Some people are more prone to negative emotions than others, but everyone can choose a stone-free heart.

◉ Yesterday. Today is the best day to start living with a positive heart.

◉ Fairness. Life is sometimes unfair, but your response to life can still be a positive choice.

◉ The road others chose. The high road has less traffic.

Focus Points...

Do good, O LORD, to those who are good, to those who are
upright in heart.
PSALM 125:4 NIV

He who loves purity of heart and has grace on his lips, the
king will be his friend.
PROVERBS 22:11 NKJV

Blessed are the pure in heart, for they shall see God.
MATTHEW 5:8 NASB

The purpose of my instruction is that all the Christians
there would be filled with love that comes from a pure
heart, a clear conscience, and sincere faith.
1 TIMOTHY 1:5 NLT

what really counts

Seeing ye have purified your souls in obeying the truth
through the Spirit unto unfeigned love of the brethren, see
that ye love one another with a pure heart fervently.
1 PETER 1:22 KJV

If I can put one touch of rosy sunset in the life of any man
or woman, I shall feel that I have worked with God.

JOHN MACDONALD

The first and the great work of a Christian is about his heart.
Do not be content with seeming to do good in "outward
acts" while your heart is bad, and you are a stranger to the
greater internal duties.

JONATHAN EDWARDS

265

Relationships

An Invested Mind

> Do not conform any longer to the pattern of this world, but be transformed by the renewing of your mind. Then you will be able to test and approve what God's will is—his good, pleasing and perfect will.
>
> ROMANS 12: 2 NIV

what really counts

Some people follow the stock market. They've invested money in the market, making each day's activities of great interest to them. The numbers for Dow Jones or NASDAQ directly affect their wealth. A good day means money has earned more money; a bad day means money was lost. To keep from losing money, investors must keep tabs on what the market does. But there are other types of investing, investments that are not measured in dollars or stock points. These are investments of time, of love, of wisdom, and of participation. Such investments require the same diligence as those made in companies and come with shares of stock.

Life is investment. Every day we deposit our lives in our businesses, work, entertainment, friends, and family. Investing our hearts and minds in our families is a work that lives on for generations, sometimes longer. It matters how and in what we invest ourselves. This is especially true for our families. Billy Graham said, "The family was ordained by God before he established any other institution, even before he established the church."

Some assume that providing a nice home, a safe environment, warmth, and food is the ultimate in family investment, but more is needed. We invest ourselves, our hearts, our minds, and, most of all, our spiritual values into those around us, our children, and our mates. Family has fallen on hard times of late, taking second place to career or personal happiness. As we go through life, we learn. Sometimes we learn from our mistakes; other times we learn from positive experiences. The lessons that are passed on to those around us are an investment of our minds.

We are the product of someone else's investment, and life demands that we pass on the favor. Not everyone will listen. Children are slow to take advice, but seeds planted now can lead to a great harvest later. God has given us minds to learn, a Bible to know, the Holy Spirit to guide us. What we learn should be invested in others, especially in family. Wisdom shared helps forge the future. The spiritual mind is never complete if it does not share what it has learned. A renewed mind is one changed by God and portrayed before those close to us. Every day is an opportunity to learn, to mature, and to renew our minds and hearts; and every day is an opportunity to share what we have learned.

Relationships
An Invested Mind

What Matters Most...

◎ Learning to learn. One of God's great gifts is the human mind.

◎ Learning to share what has been learned. Learn from others, and teach them in exchange.

◎ Knowing what is truly important. The greatest knowledge is centered upon God.

◎ Possessing a mind that is hungry for knowledge and a heart that is thirsty for wisdom.

◎ Investing in the family is investing in the future of the world.

What Doesn't Matter...

◎ Diplomas. Formal education is wonderful and desirable, but many of life's lessons occur outside the classroom.

◎ Knowing everything. No one does. What matters is sharing what you do know.

◎ Admitting ignorance. It's one of the signs of wisdom.

◎ Worldly thinking. All true change and knowledge is ultimately spiritual.

◎ Time. Everyone gets the same number of hours in the day. What you do with the hours makes the difference.

Focus Points...

You know when I sit and when I rise; you perceive my thoughts from afar. You discern my going out and my lying down; you are familiar with all my ways.
PSALM 139:2–3 NIV

The word of God is living and powerful, and sharper than any two-edged sword, piercing even to the division of soul and spirit, and of joints and marrow, and is a discerner of the thoughts and intents of the heart.
HEBREWS 4:12 NKJV

Dear friends who belong to God and are bound for heaven, think about this Jesus whom we declare to be God's Messenger and High Priest.
HEBREWS 3:1 NLT

Let no man deceive himself. If any man among you thinks that he is wise in this age, he must become foolish, so that he may become wise.
1 CORINTHIANS 3:18 NASB

If a man think himself to be something, when he is nothing, he deceiveth himself.
GALATIANS 6:3 KJV

what really counts

Change your thoughts and you will change your world.
NORMAN VINCENT PEALE

The mind is its own place, and in itself can make a heaven of hell, a hell of heaven.
JOHN MILTON

What Matters Most to Me About
Relationships

Relationships are some of the greatest treasures you have. Wealthy is the person who has true friends and a loving family. Usually you get back what you give. Relationships require that you invest yourself in the lives of others.

Having a smooth heart requires personal honesty. It requires the ability to look at not only your actions but your thoughts. Such honesty isn't always easy, but it is necessary. Write down several areas of your life where you could show more love, patience, and understanding.

_____

_____

what
really
counts _____

_____

_____

_____

Choose one area of your life in which you can improve how you relate to others. It might be at work or at home. It might be in your attitude or in your language. Pick one and list three things you are determined to do and not do that will improve the situation.

_____

_____

_____

_____

_____

◉ *The saying "A mind is a terrible thing to waste" is a true statement. The ability to think is a tremendous gift and one not to be wasted. List three things that you could do to improve your spiritual knowledge, and then list three things you could do to improve your general knowledge.*

_____

_____

_____

_____

_____

_____

_____

_____

◉ *Wisdom and knowledge go hand in hand. Knowledge tells you what can be done; wisdom tells you what should be done. Wisdom takes practice. Pick a person whom you consider to be wise and ask yourself, "What is he doing that I am not?"*

_____

_____

_____

_____

_____

_____

_____

Only the heart knows how to find what is precious.

FYODOR DOSTOYEVSKY

Significance

An Introduction

> Paul looked straight at the Sanhedrin and said, "My brothers, I have fulfilled my duty to God in all good conscience to this day."
>
> Acts 23:1 NIV

what really counts

At one of the U.S. Naval bases in California, researchers test the effects of pressure at great ocean depths. The deeper one goes into the ocean, the greater the pressure, and that pressure can be a great danger. In one test, a polystyrene cup was put under the same pressure found at the bottom of the ocean. When the test was finished, the three-inch-tall cup was no bigger than a thimble. All the air and open spaces had been compressed until only a tiny cup remained. The cup was good for nothing except to start conversations.

Life has its own pressures. At times work, family, health, and other concerns can squeeze us until we feel that we have become like that cup: smaller and useless. But there are two qualities that help the person of faith endure such hardships: obedience and perseverance.

Obedience to God is freeing. Knowing what is right in His sight and doing it bring not only satisfaction but also confidence and strength. Perseverance is the power to withstand outside pressure without being crushed. That ability is a spiritual skill given by God. Both are choices.

Life is certain to have times of confusion and heaviness. It is part of living. Some experience this more than others, unfair as that might be. How we go through such times is a mark of our significance and a testimony about our reliance upon God and the strength He has given us. Obedience and perseverance are two qualities that can change a life and change the world.

> That thou are happy, owe to God; that thou continuest such, owe to thyself, that is, to thy obedience.
>
> JOHN MILTON

Significance
Obedience: What's in a Word?

Everyone has heard about your obedience, so I am full of joy over you; but I want you to be wise about what is good, and innocent about what is evil.
ROMANS 16:19 NIV

what really counts

Our language contains many shocking words. Many of them are just four letters long. There's a much longer word that makes some people uncomfortable: *obedience*. We don't much like that word. Something about it sets us on edge. We expect children to be obedient to parents, but we feel that once we reach adulthood obedience no longer applies to us. After all, we send dogs to obedience school, and we're not dogs. A pastor was conducting a wedding rehearsal and came to the vows. After hearing the vows spoken aloud, the bride looked at the minister and asked, "Do I really have to say *obey?*"

Yet *obedience* is a powerful, biblical term. It is life-changing, exhilarating, and freeing. That's right, freeing. Bondage is the result of disobedience; liberty is the product of obedience. It is odd that obedience is seen as a sign of weakness or as an inability to think for oneself. This is especially true when we realize that Jesus was the most obedient man who ever lived. His obedience was demonstrated on the cross. It was a choice He made. This is the heart of obedience—willingness. Obedience is at its best when it arises voluntarily.

Most of us first encounter obedience when it is forced upon us. As children we are told to clean our rooms, be home by a certain time, study hard, and do our chores, and we have very little to say about it. Obedience that is chosen, however, is different. There is motivation behind it, a motivation that is "other"-based. Jesus was obedient to the point of death for our benefit, and it was through His obedience that our salvation, our connection to God, came to be.

Obedience is not the surrendering of mind or reason; it is the act of embracing the will of Someone who knows better and who has our interests at heart. Obedience is the act of "hearing" God and following His will. That direction comes through prayer, worship, and Bible study. God calls us to obedience to free us, not to bind us. Obeying is a choice that begins first in the heart. It is the submitting of ourselves and our wills so that we may grow in faith and service. *Obedience* is not a dirty word; it is a word that describes a loving, living choice. Our obedience is God's due and our privilege, and it empowers us to be more than we can imagine.

Significance
Obedience: What's in a Word?

What Matters Most...

- ◎ Knowing that God calls for obedience for your benefit. It is not a selfish act.

- ◎ Redefining obedience to understand it the way God does.

- ◎ Seeing that *obedience* isn't a dirty word but an empowering term.

- ◎ Remembering that the most obedient person to have walked the earth was Jesus.

- ◎ Understanding that obedience should never be confused with weakness.

What **Doesn't** Matter...

- ◎ The world's definition of obedience. Obedience is more than most people realize and nothing like what most people assume.

- ◎ Previous disobedience. There is always opportunity to serve God.

- ◎ Pride. Pride is the enemy of obedience and not nearly so valuable as it seems.

- ◎ Words. Words of commitment are easy to say, but actions of commitment require obedience.

- ◎ Ego. God-centered has always been better than self-centered.

Focus Points...

Being found in appearance as a man, he humbled himself and became obedient to death—even death on a cross!
PHILIPPIANS 2:8 NIV

Has the LORD as great delight in burnt offerings and sacrifices, as in obeying the voice of the LORD? Behold, to obey is better than sacrifice, and to heed than the fat of rams.
1 SAMUEL 15:22 NKJV

As through the one man's disobedience the many were made sinners, even so through the obedience of the One the many will be made righteous.
ROMANS 5:19 NASB

Having been perfected, He became the author of eternal salvation to all who obey Him.
HEBREWS 5:9 NKJV

what really counts

Obey God because you are his children. Don't slip back into your old ways of doing evil; you didn't know any better then.
1 PETER 1:14 NLT

The golden rule for understanding in spiritual matters is not intellect, but obedience.

OSWALD CHAMBERS

I was not born to be free. I was born to adore and to obey.
C. S. LEWIS

277

Significance
Perseverance Makes a Difference

Let us not lose heart in doing good, for in due time we will reap if we do not grow weary.

GALATIANS 6:9 NASB

what really counts

Someone once said, "No good deed goes uncriticized." Anyone who lives a life with goals, aspirations, and the desire to do good for others will agree. Wherever something noble is attempted, there is someone waiting to criticize or throw obstacles in the way. It's enough to make a person ask if doing good deeds is worth the effort. It is. Continuing forward is a function of perseverance. Perseverance is the determined continuation of effort in the face of setbacks, difficulties, and ridicule. The problem with perseverance is that it is easier to define than it is to do.

Perseverance is one of the hallmarks of faith. Energized by belief, we can push upward no matter how steep the grade. "Triumph," the country wise man said, "is just 'umph' added to 'try.'" What do you suppose a farmer sees when he gazes over an open, barren field? He sees opportunity. While we might see rough, rocky ground, he sees green fields. He does not fool himself. He also sees the work involved, the sweat that will come, the battles with weather and insects, but he continues on, driven by what he can achieve if he doesn't give up. The antidote to discouragement is constantly seeing what perseverance will bring. Seeing what "can be" enables us to endure "what is."

Some think that life is easier and safer if nothing great is ever attempted. Will Rogers had a different idea. He said, "Even if you are on the right track, you'll get run over if you just sit there." Perseverance is not only staying on the right track, but it is also moving forward. Perseverance is made from two ingredients: patience and endurance. *Patience* is the ability to wait without losing heart. *Endurance* is the power to withstand outside pressure. Mixed together they form the powerful, empowering force called persistence. Persistence was a hallmark of Jesus' life. No man received more criticism than He, but He never let the negative words or verbal attacks divert Him from His ministry.

Calvin Coolidge said, "Nothing in the world can take the place of persistence. Talent will not; nothing is more common than unsuccessful men with great talent. Genius will not; unrewarded genius is almost a proverb. Education will not; the world is full of educated derelicts. Persistence and determination alone are omnipotent." No matter how tired, frustrated, how uncertain, how uncomfortable—don't give in; don't give up.

Significance
Perseverance Makes a Difference

What Matters Most...

- ◎ Possessing a belief worth enduring hardship for.

- ◎ Endurance, the ability to hold up under criticism and the pressure of the world.

- ◎ Always remembering that Jesus persevered for your benefit. He's your example.

- ◎ Patience. Problems are seldom solved overnight. Persistence requires the strength of patience.

- ◎ Perseverance. Faithful determination is never done alone; God stands by your side.

What **Doesn't** Matter...

- ◎ Naysayers. Critics abound. Focus on those who can help, not on those who detract.

- ◎ Problems. Everyone has them, and the future holds more. The measure of faith is not in how few problems you have but in how you deal with them.

- ◎ Failure. Failure is just the tutor that teaches you what not to do.

- ◎ Personal wisdom. Good as that is, your wisdom must be rooted in God's wisdom.

- ◎ Fear. Fear never advances your cause; it just weighs you down.

Focus Points...

My dear brothers, stand firm. Let nothing move you. Always give yourselves fully to the work of the Lord, because you know that your labor in the Lord is not in vain.
1 CORINTHIANS 15:58 NIV

Though he fall, he shall not be utterly cast down; for the LORD upholds him with His hand.
PSALM 37:24 NKJV

I am confident of this very thing, that He who began a good work in you will perfect it until the day of Christ Jesus.
PHILIPPIANS 1:6 NASB

Who will render to every man according to his deeds: To them who by patient continuance in well doing seek for glory and honour and immortality, eternal life.
ROMANS 2:6–7 KJV

what really counts

I say to the rest of you, dear brothers and sisters, never get tired of doing good.
2 THESSALONIANS 3:13 NLT

Never give in, never give in, never, never, never, never—in nothing, great or small, large or petty—never give in except to convictions of honor and good sense.
WINSTON CHURCHILL

Persistent people begin their success where others end in failures.
EDWARD EGGLESTON

What Matters Most to Me About
Significance

To have significance in this life you must live beyond yourself. Living for God requires obedience and perseverance—companion skills that grant perspective and purpose to the things you do.

◎ Obedience *is a word that few like. It smacks of inferiority. Having seen that Christ was obedient to the point of going to the cross and did so for your benefit should change your mind. Think of three advantages of obedience and write them down.*

_____

_____

_____

_____

_____

_____

◎ *It is easy to say that you should be obedient in every area of your life, but where should you begin? That varies per individual. Jot down three areas of your life where you can develop more godly obedience.*

_____

_____

_____

_____

_____

what
really
counts

Perseverance is forged in difficulty. It takes time to learn and practice. God enables you to persevere, but the ultimate decision is yours. Think back to a time when you had to persevere through a difficult situation. What did you do right? What would you do over if you could? Write down some of your answers.

_____

_____

_____

_____

_____

_____

_____

_____

Perseverance includes patience. Patience is almost a lost art. In a world of immediate gratification, you want everything done immediately. God takes His time. Are you feeling impatient with God? If so, write down what it is you are struggling with. Then take each item to God in prayer.

_____

_____

_____

_____

_____

_____

_____

_____

The difference between perseverance and obstinacy is, that one often comes from a strong will, and the other from a strong won't.

HENRY WARD BEECHER

WORK AND CAREER

An Introduction

> Man goeth forth unto his work and to his labour until the evening.
>
> PSALM 104:23 KJV

what really counts

The alarm clock brings out honest emotion. For some, the alarm solicits a "Good morning, God!" Others start off with, "Good grief, it's morning." Our response is often tied to our work. An exciting, challenging job often propels us from bed, ready to meet new challenges. With jobs we hate it's hard to find reason to crawl out of bed. In either case, attitude—especially spiritual attitude—makes a big difference.

Work is called work because it is hard. Some work taxes the mind; other work wearies the body; some work does both. Work conditions, fellow employees, challenges of business, competition, and a hundred other things can put the pressure to us, and we begin to ask, "What next?" Some plug along grumbling under their breath and wishing they were elsewhere. Almost every adult has felt that way.

Is there more to the work we do than what we see? The Bible teaches that there is. We work not just for ourselves, but also for our God. And God is a worker as well. When we apply a spiritual perspective to hours spent at the plant or in the office, our attitude changes. No matter what you do for a living, there is a way to work for a higher calling, a higher cause.

The key is prayerful thought and opening new eyes. Many people have learned that they can do more than take a paycheck away from their work; they can take something vital to it.

Pray with all your might for the blessings in God, but work at the same time with all diligence, with all patience, with all perseverance. Pray, then, and work. Work and pray. And still again pray, and then work.

GEORGE MÜLLER

Work and Career
Whatever Your Hand Finds to Do

> Whatever your hand finds to do,
> do it with all your might.
> ECCLESIASTES 9:10 NIV

what really counts

We are created beings, made in the image of our Maker. The first time we find God mentioned in the Bible we find Him working. Genesis 1:1 reads, "In the beginning God created the heavens and the earth" (NASB). Interesting that of all the possible ways to begin the Bible, God chose to emphasize His work. As people created in His image, we have the same work nature. Work is a natural function of being human. Yet for many, work is drudgery, something that must be done to fend off starvation. Admittedly, not all work is easy or pleasant, but work can be noble.

Perhaps the problem rests in the way we look at work. Some people see leisure as a sign of success. To them, being free of the obligation of work is the ultimate goal. But as some unknown philosopher noted, "The only place where success comes before work is in the dictionary." King Solomon was the wisest man to have lived. In his heyday he was a man of keen insight. "A man can do nothing better," he wrote, "than to eat and drink and find satisfaction in his work. This too, I see, is from the hand of God, for without him, who can eat or find enjoyment?" (Ecclesiastes 2:24–25 NIV). For Solomon, work was something that brought satisfaction. If a person could be happy in his or her work, then that person was truly blessed.

Solomon says what we need to see: that work is spiritual. Regardless of what we do with our hands—clean the house, invent a new technology, rock a baby in its crib, cure a disease, drive a nail, or sweep a floor—it can be done to the glory of God. Solomon wrote more about work than anyone else in the Bible. He knew its good and bad sides, its ups and its downs. His ultimate conclusion was that work done for God was work that was meaningful.

Working for God doesn't mean showing up at church offices every morning. Any work we do, when done to God's glory, is work done for Him. That is why Solomon wrote that whatever our hands find to do, we should do with all our might. Work, career, even hobbies should be seen in the context of faith. We work not only for a living, but also for a loving. What makes work meaningful is the way we do it.

Work and Career
Whatever Your Hand Finds to Do

What Matters Most...

◎ Knowing that work doesn't bring honor to you; that you bring honor to work.

◎ Understanding that there is more to work than finishing a task and drawing a paycheck.

◎ Remembering that God is a worker and that all of creation is the product of His effort.

◎ Doing your work as if it were God who hired you.

◎ Finding your skills and desires and making them your work.

What Doesn't Matter...

◎ What others think of the type of work you do; what matters is God's view.

◎ Glory. Society esteems some work as nobler than other work, but God looks at the worker.

◎ Dreams. Dreams are good and useful, but they mean nothing unless followed by work.

◎ Constant work. Rest is part of God's program. Work hard, work smart, rest well.

◎ Praise. Praise and recognition are wonderful, but satisfaction comes from within.

Focus Points...

Six days you shall labor, but on the seventh day you shall rest; even during the plowing season and harvest you must rest.
Exodus 34:21 NIV

In everything I showed you that by working hard in this manner you must help the weak and remember the words of the Lord Jesus, that He Himself said, "It is more blessed to give than to receive."
Acts 20:35 NASB

Let him that stole steal no more: but rather let him labour, working with his hands the thing which is good, that he may have to give to him that needeth.
Ephesians 4:28 KJV

This should be your ambition: to live a quiet life, minding your own business and working with your hands, just as we commanded you before.
1 Thessalonians 4:11 NLT

what really counts

Whatever you can do or dream you can, begin it. Boldness has genius, power, and magic in it.
JOHANN WOLFGANG VON GOETHE

Far and away the best prize that life offers is the chance to work hard at work worth doing.
THEODORE ROOSEVELT

Work and Career
More Than What You Do

> The LORD said to Samuel, "Do not consider his appearance or his height, for I have rejected him. The LORD does not look at the things man looks at. Man looks at the outward appearance, but the LORD looks at the heart."
>
> 1 SAMUEL 16:7 NIV

what really counts

Just is an awful word. Walk into a restaurant alone and the hostess is likely to greet you with, "Just one this evening?" as if one is somehow less important than two. When meeting new people we ask, "What do you do for a living?" Too often the reply includes the word *just*. "Oh, I'm just a housewife . . . just a bank teller . . . just a middle executive . . ." It's a sad way to look at ourselves and our careers. Roger Ailes, a television executive and author of *You Are the Message,* says that people form their opinions of us in the first seven seconds after being introduced. Seven seconds! And very often, what we think of ourselves will come out in those few moments.

With God there is no such thing as "just" a person. He sees everything about us and in us. More than that, He sees beyond us into what we can be. The world likes to compartmentalize people. There are professionals and trades; people and laborers; college graduates and graduate-school alumni;

those who work with their hands and those who work with their minds. Even within professions some areas are seen as more prestigious than others. Cardiac surgeons garner more respect than podiatrists. These divisions are artificial. We enter the world the same; we exit the same.

Rabbi Zusya said, "In the world to come I shall not be asked, 'Why were you not Moses?' but God will ask me, 'Why were you not Zusya?'" God's value system is different from what we encounter in the world. Survey the leaders God called into service. He drew from the ranks of shepherds, fishermen, and farmers. What made the likes of David, Solomon, Elijah, Daniel, Peter, and Paul great was not the way the world looked at them, but the way God looked at them—and the way they viewed God.

Tomorrow you might be one of those who perform surgery or run on a professional football field; or you might be a mother who nurses a child, a carpenter who drives a nail, a janitor that sweeps the floor. It doesn't matter what your career makes of you; what matters is what you make of your life and what you do with what God has given you. We are more than what we do. We are what God made us, and it is in that we must excel.

Work and Career
More Than What You Do

What Matters Most...

◎ Knowing what God wants you to be and becoming it.

◎ Knowing your gifts and using them.

◎ Living up to the potential God has placed in you. You have a unique purpose.

◎ Finding your value in God's opinion and not in those around you.

◎ Believing in God, which frees you to believe in yourself.

What Doesn't Matter...

◎ The world's compartments. Grow to your gifts and potential.

◎ The word *just*. It's just a word.

◎ Income. God doesn't judge you on your bank account, but on the riches in your heart.

◎ Prestige. You are famous when you are loved by God and by those around you.

◎ Social status. There is nothing wrong with being admired by others, but it is better to be respected by God. God's value system is different from what you encounter in the world.

Focus Points...

Stop judging by mere appearances, and make a right judgment.
JOHN 7: 24 NIV

Do you look at things according to the outward appearance? If anyone is convinced in himself that he is Christ's, let him again consider this in himself, that just as he is Christ's, even so we are Christ's.
2 CORINTHIANS 10:7 NKJV

O LORD, You have searched me and known me. You know when I sit down and when I rise up; You understand my thought from afar. You scrutinize my path and my lying down, and are intimately acquainted with all my ways.
PSALM 139:1–3 NASB

People may be pure in their own eyes, but the LORD examines their motives.
PROVERBS 16:2 NLT

I the LORD search the heart, I try the reins, even to give every man according to his ways, and according to the fruit of his doings.
JEREMIAH 17:10 KJV

what really counts

He that respects himself is safe from others; he wears a coat of mail that none can pierce.

HENRY WADSWORTH LONGFELLOW

I'm a slow walker, but I never walk backwards.

ABRAHAM LINCOLN

What Matters Most to Me About
Work and Career

Most people have to work for a living or are dependent upon someone else who does. Work can be taxing, trying, boring, frustrating, and more; it can also be a place to minister, to grow, to learn, and to make a difference.

◎ *It's Monday morning, and the alarm has just gone off. How do you feel? Are you eager to face the day? Or would you rather pull the covers over your head? Below write your responses to "My work makes me feel . . ."*

_____

_____

_____

_____

what
really
counts

_____

_____

◎ *"Attitude," someone said, "is the mind's paintbrush; it can color any situation." If you are unhappy with your work, what can you change in your attitude to make it better? List a few ideas to think about.*

_____

_____

_____

_____

_____

_____

◎ *What do you love to do? If you could have any career in the world, what would it be? List a few ideas and then ask, "What's keeping me from trying?" List those as well.*

_____

_____

_____

_____

_____

_____

_____

_____

◎ *Faith touches every area of life. When working, the Bible says you should work as if it is God who hired you. List three or four things you can do to improve your work as if it were God signing your paycheck.*

_____

_____

_____

_____

_____

_____

_____

_____

Do you see a man skilled in his work? He will stand before kings; he will not stand before obscure men.
PROVERBS 22:29 NASB

Money and Wealth

An Introduction

> A rich man may be wise in his own eyes, but a poor man who has discernment sees through him.
>
> PROVERBS 28:11 NIV

what really counts

As a young lawyer Abraham Lincoln was approached by a wealthy man to help settle a dispute. The rich man had loaned $2.50 to a poor neighbor, and now he wanted his money back. Unfortunately, the neighbor couldn't pay, so the rich man wanted to retain Lincoln's services to sue.

Lincoln took the case and charged the man $10.00 in advance. Lincoln then gave the poor man $5.00 and instructed him to pay back the loan. He did and was able to keep the remaining $2.50 for himself. The rich man got his $2.50 back and the loan was cleared; the poor man fulfilled his obligation and had additional money to show for it; and Lincoln made a $5.00 fee.

The story reveals much about people's attitudes toward money. The rich man lost more than he gained, but his pride was satisfied. Since Lincoln didn't mind sharing, he was able to solve the problem without going to court. Money makes some people do strange things. There have been get-rich-quick gurus who have suggested that their students pin pictures of the things they want to the ceiling over their beds so that when they wake up, their first thought will be about that boat or house or car or vacation or whatever it is that motivates them.

Money is a tool. It is empowering, vital, and important, but it is not life. The proper perspective of wealth can bring greater happiness than wealth itself.

Money is either our master or our slave.

LATIN PROVERB

Money and Wealth
The Trials of Money

> I pray also that the eyes of your heart may be enlightened in order that you may know the hope to which he has called you, the riches of his glorious inheritance in the saints.
>
> EPHESIANS 1:18 NIV

what really counts

No area affects us, tempts us, or troubles us more than money. We live in a society where money speaks, where money is the driving force of all decisions made. Money is what enables us to get the things we need or want. Money is what most people strive for. We think it is money that will make us happy. Many people have a longing to be rich. Benjamin Franklin once wrote, "Money never made a man happy yet, nor will it. There is nothing in its nature to produce happiness. The more a man has, the more he wants. Instead of filling a vacuum, it makes one. If it satisfies one want, then it doubles and triples that want another way."

There is nothing evil about money itself. Several people in the Bible were rich: Job, Abraham, David, Solomon, and more. Money is just a device, but it still seizes the mind. Infomercials offer riches through the Internet, real estate, and other means. Millions are spent by millions wanting to make millions. The problem is, as author Henry L. Mencken noted, "The chief value of money lies in the fact that one lives in a world in which it is overestimated."

Money is viewed as either the source of problems or the solution to problems. In truth, it is neither. Income is a necessary part of life. Acquiring wealth is no sin. Depending on wealth for happiness is risky. A London newspaper offered a prize for the best definition of money. The winning entry came from one of the wealthiest men in England. His definition was, "Money is an article which may be used as a universal passport to everywhere except heaven, and as a universal provider of everything except happiness!"

In one of his letters, the apostle Paul was writing about money and said, "I am not saying this because I am in need, for I have learned to be content whatever the circumstances. I know what it is to be in need, and I know what it is to have plenty. I have learned the secret of being content in any and every situation, whether well fed or hungry, whether living in plenty or in want. I can do everything through him who gives me strength" (Philippians 4:11–13 NIV). Contentment is the key. Contentment isn't surrendering to the present circumstance; it is choosing to be happy despite the circumstance. Whether you are rich or poor, happiness is a choice.

Money and Wealth
The Trials of Money

What Matters Most...

◎ Attitude. Rejoice no matter what your condition. Grumbling never made anything better.

◎ Thanking God for the wealth you have. You may have more than you realize.

◎ Remembering that everything is temporary. Death cares nothing about bank accounts.

◎ Contentment. Contentment is a choice that overshadows your situation.

What Doesn't Matter...

◎ Physical possessions. There's no sin in possessions, but they do not bring ultimate happiness. You need God for that.

◎ Wealth. Rich people have the same spiritual needs as poor people, and they have more responsibility to use their wealth for the good of others.

◎ Poverty. A poor bank account doesn't make for a poor person. Great men and women have worked through poverty.

◎ Pride. Wealth can lead to an unjustified ego, which can render a wealthy person rich in property and poor in spirit.

◎ Opinions other than God's. Poverty has never made anyone ashamed in God's presence.

Focus Points...

The love of money is a root of all kinds of evil. Some people, eager for money, have wandered from the faith and pierced themselves with many griefs.
1 Timothy 6:10 NIV

He who loves silver will not be satisfied with silver; nor he who loves abundance, with increase. This also is vanity.
Ecclesiastes 5:10 NKJV

No one can serve two masters; for either he will hate the one and love the other, or he will be devoted to one and despise the other. You cannot serve God and wealth.
Matthew 6:24 NASB

Stay away from the love of money; be satisfied with what you have. For God has said, "I will never fail you. I will never forsake you."
Hebrews 13:5 NLT

what really counts

Wealth and riches shall be in his house: and his righteousness endureth for ever.
Psalm 112:3 KJV

Get all you can, save all you can, and give all you can.
John Wesley

The poorest man I know is the man who has nothing but money.
John D. Rockefeller Jr.

Money and Wealth
Wealth and Happiness

> Instruct those who are rich in this present world not to be conceited or to fix their hope on the uncertainty of riches, but on God, who richly supplies us with all things to enjoy.
>
> 1 TIMOTHY 6:17 NASB

what really counts

One of the great Broadway musicals that was later made into a movie is *Fiddler on the Roof.* In it, a poor Jewish man in Russia sings the poignant but cheery "If I Were a Rich Man." In the song, he intones about how his life would be different if he were just a little rich. He had a belief that happiness comes from wealth—material wealth. Many people believe the same thing. The Bible does not condemn people who own wealth; it does, however, condemn those who allow wealth to own them.

Older volumes of the *Guinness Book of World Records* list Hettie Green (1835–1916) as the world's stingiest miser. According to the account, she lived on cold oatmeal because she didn't want to spend the money to heat it. She had deposited in just one bank 31.4 million dollars, an enormous amount of money even by today's standards. Yet, despite having such enviable wealth, her son's leg had to be amputated because of the time lost trying to find *free* medical help after he was injured. When she died, she left an estate of $95 million. Few would argue that something was very wrong. Whatever the cause, wealth owned her more than she owned her wealth.

Scholar William Boice said this in prayer: "Dear Lord, I have been re-reading the record of the Rich Young Ruler and his obviously wrong choice. But it has set me thinking. No matter how much wealth he had, he could not ride in a car, have any surgery, turn on a light, buy penicillin, hear a pipe organ, watch TV, wash dishes in running water, type a letter, mow a lawn, fly in an airplane, sleep on an innerspring mattress, or talk on the phone. If he was rich, then what am I?" His point is well taken: Most of us are far richer than we realize.

Happiness comes from within and from above. There are powerful people who are miserable, famous people who are lonely, wealthy people who live without peace. Wealth is a wonderful tool, but it is not the key that unlocks the doors of contentment. That takes a spiritual commitment. To paraphrase Dr. Chuck Swindoll, "Money can buy medicine but not health, a house but not a home, companionship but not friends, entertainment but not happiness, food but not an appetite, a bed but not sleep, a crucifix but not a Savior, a good life but not eternal life."

Money and Wealth
Wealth and Happiness

What Matters Most...

◎ Priorities. Monetary wealth is great, but it is a pale comparison to spiritual wealth.

◎ Being the owner; not the owned. It is fine for you to take hold of financial wealth, but it must never take hold of you.

◎ Understanding that happiness comes from within and from above, never from without.

◎ Focus. Only God is worthy to sit on the throne of your life. Wealth can never do for you what He has done.

◎ Remembering that the most valuable things in life can't be banked. Salvation, family, friends, hope, humor, and a thousand more intangibles are better than wealth.

What Doesn't Matter...

◎ Bank statements in heaven. God has never said, "Sorry, you're too poor."

◎ The treadmill. Chasing wealth often leaves the pursuer disappointed.

◎ The question "Why?" Everyone is born into a different situation. What matters is where you go from there.

◎ How the rich live. Envy moves no one forward, but prayerful action does.

◎ Complaining. Poverty is no joy, but it has never been changed by complaining. Pray, chart a course, get busy.

Focus Points...

The trustworthy will get a rich reward. But the person who wants to get rich quick will only get into trouble.
PROVERBS 28:20 NLT

Jesus said to his disciples, "I tell you the truth, it is hard for a rich man to enter the kingdom of heaven."
MATTHEW 19:23 NIV

Do not be afraid when one becomes rich, when the glory of his house is increased; for when he dies he shall carry nothing away; his glory shall not descend after him.
PSALM 49:16–17 NKJV

He who trusts in his riches will fall, but the righteous will flourish like the green leaf.
PROVERBS 11:28 NASB

what really counts

I say unto you, Take no thought for your life, what ye shall eat, or what ye shall drink; nor yet for your body, what ye shall put on. Is not the life more than meat, and the body than raiment?
MATTHEW 6:25 KJV

I have made many millions, but they have brought me no happiness. I would barter them all for the day I sat on an office stool in Cleveland and counted myself rich on three dollars a week.

JOHN D. ROCKEFELLER

There is nothing wrong with people possessing riches. The wrong comes when riches possess people.

BILLY GRAHAM

What Matters Most to Me About
Money and Wealth

Money is a necessity of life. Wealth is both a blessing and a burden. Poverty is a desperate challenge. Money and wealth are also very misunderstood. A proper and balanced view of money can bring pleasure to your life and glory to God.

◎ *Since wealth is no guarantee of happiness, what is? What gives you the greatest pleasure in life? In what do you find satisfaction? In the space below, list several items that matter most to you. Ask, "What is really important?"*

_____

_____

_____

_____

_____

_____

◎ *Money comes with a price. With noble, important causes, the price is worth paying, but too often people work hard for things they don't really need or want. Finish the sentence "My money costs me . . ." Study your list and ask if changes need to be made.*

_____

_____

_____

_____

_____

what
really
counts

⊙ *It is said that if you want to feel rich, then count all the blessings you have that money can't buy. List below a few items, relationships, or situations that you value but that can't be bought with money.*

_____

_____

_____

_____

_____

_____

_____

_____

⊙ *There is a human tendency to compare ourselves to others who have more. Consider comparing yourself to those who have less. How does that change your perspective?*

_____

_____

_____

_____

_____

_____

_____

_____

Too many people spend money they haven't earned to buy things they don't want, to impress people they don't like.
WILL ROGERS

HEALTH

An Introduction

> In those days Hezekiah became ill and was at the point of death. He prayed to the LORD, who answered him and gave him a miraculous sign.
>
> 2 CHRONICLES 32:24 NIV

what really counts

The apostle Paul was a unique and dedicated man. When Christianity first began to spread from Jerusalem, he persecuted the believers, throwing many people in jail. Then he had an encounter with Christ. His life was forever changed, and he traveled the known world preaching the same message he had previously persecuted with vehemence. He wrote many of the New Testament books, started many churches, and preached uncounted sermons. The lives of millions were changed. You might think someone that important, powerful, influential, and spiritual would be protected from health issues. He wasn't.

Paul had a physical problem. Scholars debate what that problem was. The reason they debate it is that Paul never says what his illness is, nor does he complain about it. He does allude to it, however. Some think he had an eye disease, because in one of his letters he comments about the last few comments being in his own hand and written in large letters. Others think he suffered from malaria contracted during his travels. What his disease was is immaterial. The point is that even the greatest of individuals have health issues.

Nothing reminds us of our mortality faster than the onset of illness. No one likes to be ill, handicapped, in pain, or weak. Yet, we know that we will encounter such things. The good news is that we don't have to go through these things alone and that prayer changes things.

> We are all healers who can reach out and offer health, and we are all patients in constant need of help.
>
> HENRI NOUWEN

Health
Wonderfully Made

> You created my inmost being; you knit me together in my mother's womb. I praise you because I am fearfully and wonderfully made; your works are wonderful, I know that full well.
>
> PSALM 139:13–14 NIV

what really counts

In 1966, Isaac Asimov wrote the small novel *Fantastic Voyage*. It's the story of a surgical team placed in an atomic submarine, shrunk to a very small size, and then injected into the body of a dying man. There they encounter amazing sights as seen from inside the human body. The book, which was also a movie, still holds the attention of many people forty years later. The premise of the book is impossible, but with a little imagination it becomes believable. What an amazing trip it would be to travel through the human body. Such a traveler would never be the same.

The human anatomy is a stunning bit of creation that reminds us of our Creator. Our bodies have ten systems: skeletal, circulatory, nervous, urinary, reproductive, muscular, digestive, immune, and endocrine. The 206 bones are useless without muscles to move them; muscles would fail if the circulatory system did not feed them nutrients and oxygen;

the nervous system controls the body's operation. All of it is connected and operates together in a biological ballet we call life. The system is complicated, beyond what we could design and bring into being. No wonder the psalmist wrote, "I praise you because I am fearfully and wonderfully made" (Psalm 139:14 NIV).

One of the great dangers we face is forgetting how amazing God's creation is—and we make up just a part of His overall design. A young man had been teetering on the edge of spiritual life. He wasn't certain God existed, and yet he felt an inner urge to find God. An avid hiker and camper, he set out to spend a few days in the woods. One evening as the sun set and his campfire burned nearby, he picked a leaf from a bush and studied it. The more he looked at it, the more impressed he was with what he held. He wondered how such a leaf with its cells, veins, chlorophyll, stem, and so much more could come to be. Then he looked at his hand and wondered how something infinitely more complex came to be. Then it hit. It was not accident. There, alone in the woods, he encountered God, and his life changed forever. We are fearfully and wonderfully made, and to see that, all we have to do is take the time to look. We are no accident. The Creator who made us and the universe wants to be known.

Health
Wonderfully Made

What Matters Most...

◉ Knowing that God is an artist and that you are His art.

◉ Seeing that creation isn't something "out there." Creation is also something right here, even inside you.

◉ Understanding that the complex mechanisms of the human body remind you that you serve a thinking, creative, powerful God.

◉ Seeing the human body as miraculous evidence for a miraculous God.

◉ Being known. God knows you in detail; He knows you inside out.

What **Doesn't** Matter...

◉ Understanding how everything works. Gaining knowledge is a godly thing, but you know enough about creation to know about God.

◉ The idea that everything you see, including your body, is the result of an accident. A design requires a designer.

◉ Imperfections in the world. An imperfect world does not imply an imperfect God.

◉ Limited vision. There is more to see beyond this life. What you see is just a glimpse.

◉ Time. Today is a good day to start seeing God's fingerprints.

Focus Points...

God created man in his own image, in the image of God he created him; male and female he created them.
GENESIS 1:27 NIV

Just as you do not know the path of the wind and how bones are formed in the womb of the pregnant woman, so you do not know the activity of God who makes all things.
ECCLESIASTES 11:5 NASB

What is man, that thou art mindful of him? and the son of man, that thou visitest him? For thou hast made him a little lower than the angels, and hast crowned him with glory and honour.
PSALM 8:4–5 KJV

Acknowledge that the LORD is God! He made us, and we are his. We are his people, the sheep of his pasture.
PSALM 100:3 NLT

what really counts

The higher the mountains, the more understandable is the glory of Him who made them and who holds them in His hand.

FRANCIS SCHAEFFER

There is about us, if only we have eyes to see, a creation of such spectacular profusion, spendthrift richness, and absurd detail, as to make us catch our breath in astonished wonder.

MICHAEL MAYNE

313

Health
Faith and Illness

Do you not know that your body is a temple of the Holy Spirit who is in you, whom you have from God, and that you are not your own? For you have been bought with a price: therefore glorify God in your body.

1 CORINTHIANS 6:19–20 NASB

what really counts

A young pastor walked down one of the halls of a children's hospital. He was there to visit a child who had fallen from a slowly moving car. Fortunately, the child received only minor injuries. As he walked, the pastor kept his head down and his eyes fixed to the highly polished floor. On both sides were the open doors of patient rooms. He didn't look in. He was afraid of what he might see: children hooked to machines, frightened parents keeping noble vigil at bedsides. After his visit and after prayer, the pastor retraced his steps. This time he confronted his fear. He paused and looked in doors, smiled at pale and frail children, nodded at parents. When he left he had no more answers than when he arrived, but he knew he could face the illness of others.

No matter how careful we are, how much we exercise, how vigilant we are about diet, we face illness. It's an unpleasant topic. Many people go through life thinking heart attacks are tragedies that happen to others, that pneumonia, cancer, and similar afflictions hit the "other guy." But the day comes when we become the other guy. It was true in Jesus' day. Much of Jesus' ministry was to the sick, healing everything from leprosy to blindness. Without modern medicine, the people of Jesus' day faced an early death and frequent illnesses.

Faith applies to everything and at every time, even during illness. Faith connects us to the God who can heal, or if healing isn't in His will, faith can empower us to endure illness. Mindy was a wonderful, godly woman who spent much of her adult life battling crippling arthritis. Her hands were twisted, and the disease had settled in her spine. She was often in pain, but she always wore a smile and had a compliment or praise at the ready. From time to time, well-meaning but misinformed people would tell her that if she "only had more faith," God would heal her. God never did, but He did touch scores of lives through the woman who never let her disease cripple her faith as it had crippled her hands. Her disease made her more powerful in prayer and in faith.

Illness is part of life. At times God heals the body; at other times He strengthens the soul. Whether in health or illness, God is there.

Health
Faith and Illness

What Matters Most...

◎ Knowing that illness is not unusual but that you can face it with unusual faith.

◎ Praying. Prayer has a direct impact on illness, and it often leads to healing of the body. At the very least, prayer encourages the soul.

◎ Responsibility. Living healthy is a responsibility for people of faith. It's good management of what God has given you.

◎ Praying for others when they are ill. The difference it makes is remarkable.

◎ Patience and asking. Ask for healing, but also ask to know God's will in your illness.

What Doesn't Matter...

◎ Self-pity. "Why me?" No one is exempt. Rich and poor, weak and powerful, all face illness.

◎ Fatalism. Never surrender to illness. Do everything you can to stay healthy or regain your health. Leave the rest for God.

◎ Those who say your faith is too small. Believe, trust, and wait on God.

◎ Those who say doctors are unnecessary. When sick, see a doctor. God gave you common sense.

Focus Points...

Indeed he was ill, and almost died. But God had mercy on him, and not on him only but also on me, to spare me sorrow upon sorrow.
PHILIPPIANS 2:27 NIV

The LORD will strengthen him on his bed of illness; You will sustain him on his sickbed.
PSALM 41:3 NKJV

When He entered the house, the blind men came up to Him, and Jesus said to them, "Do you believe that I am able to do this?" They said to Him, "Yes, Lord."
MATTHEW 9:28 NASB

Is any sick among you? let him call for the elders of the church; and let them pray over him, anointing him with oil in the name of the Lord.
JAMES 5:14 KJV

what really counts

To keep me from getting puffed up, I was given a thorn in my flesh, a messenger from Satan to torment me and keep me from getting proud.
2 CORINTHIANS 12:7 NLT

In time of sickness the soul collects itself anew.
LATIN PROVERB

Sickness helps to remind men of death. Sickness helps to make men think seriously of God, and their souls, and the world to come.
J. C. RYLE

317

What Matters Most to Me About
Health

No one can avoid illness forever, but there is much you can do to embrace health and to deal with illness when it comes. Faith and prayer can play an important role in your physical life.

◉ *The apostle Paul told the members of the church at Corinth that their bodies were temples for the Holy Spirit. That puts a different spin on how you look at yourself. According to the Bible, God indwells the believer. Knowing that, how should you view the body you have? Jot down a few ideas.*

_____

_____

_____

what
really
counts_____

_____

_____

_____

◉ *When you pray about an illness, you long for healing. It is good and appropriate to pray for healing, but it is also good to pray for what you need to deal with your illness: courage, strength, hope, and understanding. When ill, what three or four things do you feel you need most? Write them down.*

_____

_____

_____

_____

_____

_____

⊙ *One of the great privileges of life in faith is the opportunity to pray for others. Your prayers have an impact on their condition. Whom do you know who could benefit from your prayers? List two or three people in need of prayer for their physical condition and pray for them.*

_____

_____

_____

_____

_____

_____

_____

_____

⊙ *Faith often blooms in the darkest night. It is easy to have faith when everything goes well. Have you learned anything about yourself or about God during an illness? What things did you learn? Make a note of them below.*

_____

_____

_____

_____

_____

_____

_____

_____

If you are swept off your feet, it's time to get on your knees.

FRED BECK